The "No-Nonsense" Guide to Doing Business in Japan

Also by Jon Woronoff

ASIA'S 'MIRACLE' ECONOMIES

HONG KONG: Capitalist Paradise

INSIDE JAPAN, INC

* JAPAN AS – *ANYTHING BUT* – NUMBER ONE

* THE JAPANESE ECONOMIC CRISIS

* THE JAPANESE SOCIAL CRISIS

* JAPAN'S COMMERCIAL EMPIRE

JAPAN'S MARKET: The Distribution System (*with Michael R. Czinkota*)

JAPAN'S WASTED WORKERS

* JAPANESE TARGETING

THE JAPAN SYNDROME

KOREA'S ECONOMY: Man-Made Miracle

* POLITICS: The Japanese Way

UNLOCKING JAPAN'S MARKETS

WORLD TRADE WAR

* *From the same publishers*

The "No-Nonsense" Guide to Doing Business in Japan

Jon Woronoff

Second Edition

Published 2001 by
PALGRAVE
Houndmills, Basingstoke, Hampshire RG21 6XS and
175 Fifth Avenue, New York, N. Y. 10010
Companies and representatives throughout the world

PALGRAVE is the new global academic imprint of
St. Martin's Press LLC Scholarly and Reference Division and
Palgrave Publishers Ltd (formerly Macmillan Press Ltd).

First edition 1991
Second edition 2001

ISBN 0–333–80437–6

This book is printed on paper suitable for recycling and
made from fully managed and sustained forest sources.

A catalogue record for this book is available
from the British Library.

Library of Congress Cataloging-in-Publication Data
Woronoff, Jon.
    The "no nonsense" guide to doing business in Japan / Jon Woronoff.—
    2nd ed.
       p. cm.
    Includes bibliographical references and index.
    ISBN 0–333–80437–6 (cloth)
      1. Japan—Commerce. 2. Corporations, Foreign—Japan. I. Title: Guide to
    doing business in Japan. II. Title.

    HF3826.5 .W67 2000
    658'.049'0952—dc21
                                                          00–042210

10   9   8   7   6   5   4   3   2   1
10   09 08 07 06 05 04 03 02 01

Printed in Great Britain by Antony Rowe Ltd, Chippenham, Wiltshire

Contents

Foreword

Well, Mr Woronoff, do you really think it makes sense to produce an update to *The "No-Nonsense" Guide to Doing Business in Japan?* After all, Japan has been undergoing its most serious postwar recession, far worse than earlier ones in Europe and America. The Japanese companies, so widely and highly praised just a decade ago, have revealed terrible flaws. They are no longer the fearsome competitors they used to be nor brilliant models for everyone to copy. And the Japanese market is sluggish, trying vainly to recover.

Yes, indeed, I do. The most important reason is quite simple. Even the longest recession must come to an end and, when it does, the Japanese economy will snap back. Even in its present state, it is still the world's second biggest market, and hardly one that should be neglected. Moreover, when the Japanese companies recover they will again become fierce rivals, and their ferocity, as well as the tactics they use, can best be countered from within Japan. Now is as good a time as any, and probably better than any earlier period, to get into Japan and prepare for the future.

The update is necessary because over the past decade there have been many changes in the market situation. It is becoming increasingly feasible – but certainly not easy – to export, to set up an office, even to buy a Japanese company. Many of the formal barriers have come down and the state machinery is actually moving in the direction of greater openness. On the other hand, most of the hidden barriers, including those of a cultural nature, are still largely there and cannot be ignored. So, even though there are more successes, there are still lots of failures. And you would not want to be one of them, would you?

The need for a "no-nonsense" guide as opposed to just any guide has not really decreased. There are still those who downplay the difficulties, insisting that the market is now fully open and it just takes a bit of a push to get in. That is, after all, the view Japanese officials and companies defend, and which is taken up by Western "friends." There are also those who insist that the market is still tightly closed, and that the Japanese will use every trick to keep foreigners out. That is more than ever a case of "sour grapes," but it does not keep the view from scaring off potential rivals. And there will probably never be an end to those who peddle some magic formula or propose some unique key to the market which, when adopted by the foreign businessman, will dissolve every impediment and open every door.

Success can be facilitated, although never guaranteed, by a more realistic and balanced understanding, one considering the real opportunities and the real problems. It should concede that every company is different so no one solution will work for all. It should realize that Japan is clearly a special marketplace, but not one so different that all previous experiences elsewhere have to be discarded. And, probably most important, it should admit that Japanese culture plays a decisive role but one whose effect can be adapted to and even altered by suitable action.

Again, as ten years ago, I don't suppose I have fully achieved my goal. There is probably some information I missed, angles I failed to cover, even advice that may be questionable. But I have done my damnedest to get things right and tell it like it is. In a sense, I have finally written (and now revised) the book I wish I had read when I first arrived in Japan. I sincerely hope it helps you in your efforts to make good in what remains one of the toughest, and also one of the most attractive, markets in the world.

JON WORONOFF

1

A Different Japan?

People change, companies change, countries change. It would seem that some of the biggest changes over the past decade have occurred in Japan. At the end of the 1980s, it had the strongest economy, with the most competitive companies, manned with particularly dynamic and hardworking employees, and backed by an unusually able and supportive government. It seemed that there was no stopping Japan and the Japanese.

Unfortunately, the Japanese got carried away. They began to believe in their infallibility and sought endless expansion. Thus, some of the growth was spurious, going into excess capacity in manufacturing and excessive spending in all sectors. What Japan was creating, although hardly anyone realized at the time, was a huge "bubble." During the 1990s, that bubble burst and Japan sank into its worst postwar recession, which was actually one of the worst experienced by any modern economy.[1]

The views of Japan at present are quite different. They include a degree of *Schadenfreude*, especially among those who had earlier been beaten by the Japanese. So, it appears, Japanese businessmen, bureaucrats and politicians are not nearly as wily as thought. Indeed, they are having so much trouble coming out of the slump that they are increasingly met with contempt or pity for their ineffectual efforts at revitalizing the economy. They are told to reform, to reform like us in the West, who obviously know better. And sometimes it seems that they are doing so.

Thus, before getting down to more practical matters, it would be wise to reflect on just what has happened in Japan. First, to see

1

where the economy went wrong. Then to consider the efforts made to "fix" it. And finally to examine how much has actually changed. It may then turn out that this is not quite a different Japan, a Japan more like us, the fondest dream of all foreigners who tire of having to adjust. Instead, it will be a mixture, including a few new gimmicks borrowed from the West, but with a Japanese flavor. But the foundation will be relatively untouched, as Japanese and as unfathomable as ever to most unless they are willing to make an effort at understanding.

After this, you can move on to the essential question of how to do business in today's Japan, which is not all that very different from yesterday's.

The bubble bursts

If a day can make a big difference in a person's life, how much difference can a decade make in a country's life? Looking at it from a distance, the decade of the 1990s brought a drastic change in the situation of Japan, and especially the Japanese economy. At the end of the 1980s, it was admired as the strongest and most dynamic economy in the world. Japanese companies were expanding worldwide, buying up vast amounts of prime property and, more significantly, establishing branches around the globe and acquiring slews of foreign firms.

When meeting foreign companies in combat, the Japanese usually won out. They seemed to have every possible edge. They possessed more modern factories with more advanced technologies, they could churn out huge numbers of products renowned for their quality and yet priced so cheaply that they drove out the competition. It looked as if the Japanese were utterly demolishing their rivals in certain sectors, and might almost establish a monopoly for crucial products such as steel, ships, automobiles, consumer electronics and semiconductors. They were not only catching up on standard products, they appeared to be in the forefront for new ones in biotechnology, computers and chips, even aviation and rockets. In the services, Japanese banks, securities companies and insurance firms were among the world's largest.[2]

Yet, the crucial edge seemed to be not mere production and technology but the human element. The Japanese had the most dedicated and diligent personnel in the world, held together by a management system that foreigners sought to emulate, while realizing they could not quite achieve it. The most flourishing sector in business schools and literature was the "learn from Japan" variety. Tens, hundreds, maybe even thousands of books and reports appeared analysing every possible facet, from more technical ones like quality control and robotization to softer ones like groupism and lifetime employment.[3]

By the end of the 1990s, the view was completely different. This again applies predominantly to the economy. Economic growth – once worldbeating – had slowed to a level beneath that of most European countries, lagging particularly against a resurgent United States. The economy had actually slipped into a recession with negative growth and otherwise sluggish progress, and upturns were usually short and disappointing. This despite repeated and massive government stimulation packages. Deflation went on for most of the period and yet, no matter how much stimulation and deflation occurred, the Japanese were so worried about the future that they saved rather than spending and some despaired of the economy ever recovering. Moreover, unemployment rose to nearly 5%, the highest rate in decades.

Meanwhile, the once proud Japanese companies have come upon hard times. Profits, never especially good, have been exceedingly meager and sometimes turned into losses which, when unsustainable, resulted in record numbers of bankruptcies. Not only small and medium enterprises were in trouble, so were larger ones like Nissan, Toshiba, Mitsubishi Motors and many others.

And this was further compounded by the massive debts they had accumulated during the years of rapid expansion. Manufacturers had borrowed to build new factories and acquire foreign firms, and now that money had to be paid back with interest. But this was nothing compared to the fate of the property developers, which were stuck with severely depressed assets, or the brokerages, whose clients often bought on margin. Naturally, the banks which had loaned to all of them were stuck with enormous uncollectable debts. The figures bandied about, most smaller than reality, were mind-boggling.

As usual, Japanese industry tried to export its way out of the recession. Every effort was made to sell more steel, ships, automobiles, electronics... . But these products were no longer so competitive. European and American rivals had caught up technologically in many cases, and sometimes offered very good quality and prices. With weaker currencies, Korea, Taiwan and the other NICs could readily undercut Japan. Production for an increasing range of Japanese articles peaked and declined further from year to year, taking forever to reach a low point from which they might then rebound.

And what about Japanese management? It gradually became a laughing stock. First, the weaknesses became more evident. Most obviously, once companies stopped expanding, they were stuck with too much of everything: too many factories, that were far too big; too many models for every product, some of them not very fetching; too many suppliers, distributors and subsidiaries of every sort, many of them making losses; and above all, too many employees. In the services there was also too much, especially too much debt, and too few new ideas.

In the West, such problems had also emerged during recessions, but most Western companies were more ruthless in cutting back, closing down factories, selling off subsidiaries and laying off personnel. The Japanese had trouble doing this and thus the downturn lasted far longer. By the end of the decade no one was reading "learn from Japan" management books any more, most of the old ones had been scrapped, and newspaper articles pictured the Japanese as congenitally incapable of reform. Or, taking an opposite tack, critics proclaimed that the Japanese system was dead with the passing of lifetime employment, the corporate groups (*keiretsu*) and government guidance and assistance. Both of these contrary views were surely wrong, as wrong as much of the sillier praise of the past.

Never-ending change

On the surface, the 1990s was a decade of constant change which should make Japan a very different place in the 21st century. One after the other, businessmen, bureaucrats and politicians have been announcing reforms which revised or reversed traditional practices and should make the economy more vigorous and companies more successful. Part of this stemmed from the realization that, with the economy in a deep slump, they had been doing something wrong before and had better change. But much of the impetus came from innovations being adopted abroad, which appeared to give Western economies greater efficiency and Western companies more punch. In addition, Western governments – and particularly that of the United States – put Japan under considerable pressure to change at least those aspects of the system that worked against their own businessmen.

Thus, most of the reforms were deceptively familiar to Westerners because they took their inspiration from the West. Still, it must be remembered, while Japan is good at copying others, it almost always gives a special twist to what it borrows to make it more compatible with a very different cultural foundation. So, the reforms in Japan may not be quite the same. Moreover, most of the reforms affect "hard" aspects of the economy, those relating to rules and regulations, profits and losses, yen and sen (dollars and cents), which are easier to implement. Fewer relate to the "soft" aspects, those which most affect cultural predispositions and hangups.

Japan was under persistent foreign pressure to keep opening its market and, indeed, it has done so. The bulk of the remaining tariff barriers were reduced or eliminated, making the general tariff level lower than in most of its partners. Of course, there were a few exceptions, but very few by now. Admittedly, some of the formal tariff barriers were replaced by non-tariff barriers, various rules and regulations which kept foreigners at bay in practice. And the bureaucrats could, and did, create new hurdles or simply stall to protect Japanese companies. Still, there was a shift from export-promotion to a degree of promotion of imports, this most notably in the activities of the Japan External Trade Organization.[4]

So the next call was for deregulation, to make it easier for all, Japanese and foreigners, to get into various previously closed sectors and also to limit the possibilities of bureaucratic meddling. The most prominent was the "big bang" in the financial sector, which would facilitate competition by foreign banks, which could more readily engage in diverse activities and use their advanced techniques or cheaper price to win a clientele. Meanwhile fixed commissions would be dropped for share trading, helping foreign brokerages. But this was not all. There was also deregulation in telecommunications, housing, pharmaceuticals, energy and so on.

With heavier debts than ever, and foreign competitors ruthlessly undercutting, Japanese companies began to concentrate more on profits. The worst off had to do so simply to survive. More successful ones did this to revive the stock market and get new sources of finance. Thus, shareholder value suddenly became a buzzword. This could be enhanced in various ways. Most simply, rather than present meaningless, if not outright misleading, financial statements they adopted somewhat more accurate accounting and auditing practices, and those which were also listed abroad had no choice but to apply Western standards. The government also imposed new rules which would improve transparency and, for the first time, force companies to reveal more about the situation in their various subsidiaries.

With this, it would be much easier to engage in restructuring, another buzzword, since profitable operations could be kept and expanded while loss-making ones might be disposed of. There was even some effort at creating profit centers within the company, so each division would pull its weight. More generally, it was realized that the product line had to be slimmed down; too many different models with too many assorted options cost more than they were worth. Likewise, inefficient factories could be closed and superfluous branch offices and retail outlets consolidated. Another, rather simple, way of boosting share prices was for the company to buy back its shares, which many promptly announced they would do. And, to give managers a vested interest in improved performance and higher share prices, more dynamic companies like Kyocera launched share option schemes.

There also seemed finally to be fissures in Japan, Inc. Short of cash themselves, many companies began rejecting the (moral) obligations of aiding members of their group or *keiretsu*. They saw little point in bailing out companies which had made serious mistakes and whose liabilities they could not afford to share. Toyota even stated boldly that its own business came first and would not be subject to the interests of the broader group. Gradually, to raise cash, companies sold off shares in related firms and the cross-shareholdings began to unwind. More striking in some ways, the bureaucrats allowed struggling companies which were too indebted to collapse, even in the financial sector which had always been supported by the Ministry of Finance. The number of bankcruptcies rose implicably, a further reminder that profits must be maintained if for no other reason than to avoid going under.

As cross-shareholding and other links became weaker, and companies were willing to part with less successful operations, new opportunities opened up for mergers and acquisitions (M&A), something that had always been eschewed before. Weaker companies eagerly sought partners, even weak ones, with whom they might merge in order to save money and generate synergies, another buzzword. The amount of M&A shot up sharply among Japanese companies, and more unexpectedly there were also many cases of M&A in which foreign companies bought up or into Japanese ones. In other ways, foreign companies were made to feel more at home, finally being accepted as members of some trade associations and even the Japanese Federation of Economic Organizations (Keidanren).

There were also changes within the employment system, the soft, cultural underpinnings of Japanese business. The buzzword there was downsizing. Hundred of companies announced plans to reduce personnel by fairly large numbers and employees were warned to shape up or ship out (if not quite as crudely as abroad).

To encourage greater effort, there was a trend to base remuneration more on performance and less on seniority. Sony was particularly noticeable here. It could even happen that a younger manager would be moved to a top position without having to wait his turn. Employees were increasingly urged to learn useful skills, skills that would serve them well within the company and also outside, if they did leave.

This certainly seems like sweeping changes in Japan's corporate world. However, if you look closer, you may have a queazy feeling that …

Plus ça change …

Yes, indeed. The more things change, the more they remain the same. That, at least, is the impression one has after having witnessed repeated waves of reform which, when they receded, left only relatively minimal change behind. There was much talk and little action, with most of the action taken by the usual innovators, Sony, Toyota, Kyocera and so on. After all, most of the reforms were inspired, and sometimes imposed, by the West, so the Japanese had little interest in maintaining them and a fertile imagination when it comes to ways of getting around the rules. Thus, a closer inspection is helpful.

There is no question but that the tariff barriers, quotas and many of the non-tariff barriers have disappeared and it is certainly easier for foreigners to export, produce locally and complete in all sectors. And the deregulation was for real. For the moment at least, the bureaucrats are cooperating. But when the recovery comes and the foreign money and technology are less essential, it is possible that new hindrances will emerge and that the bureaucrats will get back to their old tricks. However, for foreign companies which have become established, this may actually be a plus since they will now be protected as well.

There is also no doubt that there is a greater interest in profitability than before. This is necessary to keep the company going and, in many cases, to pay off the crippling debts that were accumulated during the previous expansion. But the restructuring has been minimal. Relatively few companies have actually sold off weak subsidiaries or other related firms. There have been mergers, but the new entity rarely cut back radically by closing down factories, branch offices or retail outlets. Nor has there been much trimming of the staff. Rather, the two old companies almost coexisted within the new one, with just some informal coordination at the top. There were bankruptcies but, aside from some notable cases, mainly of smaller firms.

The M&A transactions involving foreigners, however, are another matter. This is a major breakthrough. For the first time foreign companies can enter the Japanese market rapidly and massively just by taking over or merging with a Japanese competitor. That opportunity is precious. But it may not be as easy, or as cheap, once the economy recovers. Also, it remains to be seen whether, once having supposedly taken over a Japanese company, the foreign managers will be able to turn the acquired firm into a united and efficient operation through restructuring, downsizing and other techniques that may work better abroad.

While the new accounting and auditing rules make it much easier for foreigners to tell the good companies from the bad, and to direct their investments more intelligently, it is far from certain the Japanese will do the same. Companies within the same group or *keiretsu* still have very close ties. Even if the overall share of cross-holding has diminished, it was not by that much and remains at about 40% or more. Any shares were usually sold in more distant or smaller firms with which preserving close relations was less important.

Of course, the emphasis on profitability has had some impact on the employment system. But speaking of the demise of "lifetime employment," as some have done, is very premature. Most of the announcements of massive layoffs were long on broad goals and short on specifics. Usually, the targets were not met; they may not even have been intended to be met but rather proffered as a sign of good will. And the reductions only took place over the years, usually by the fairly painless method of attrition. True, some companies – but not most – actually did increase the share of wages attributed to performance, but this was usually much less than the share related to seniority. And some managers were promoted on ability. But their seniors were then retired to cushy advisory posts, a rather expensive expedient.

Thus seniority has remained the basic principle and younger staff were not eager to break ranks and annoy their colleagues for the petty advantages offered. Moreover, there were so many layers of seniors above them that junior staff always faced resistance to new ideas. Meanwhile, since promotion remained largely a matter of hanging on, managers tended not to rock the boat and just sought to get by, relatively unnoticed, and to continue rising with the career escalator. The top executives had never been much interested in profits (although losses did worry them) and so they were just as happy to keep an even keel without taking risky initiatives which might (or might not) enhance profitability. Since most of the shares were still in the hands of friendly companies, run by executives of a similar disposition, they cooperated as necessary to keep disruptive (foreign) elements out of the company group and, in general, the economy. With numerous bureaucrats parachuting into post-retirement jobs with such companies, there was little chance they would support the reforms either, especially since many were clearly directed against the bureaucracy.

So, some things have changed. And it would be a great pity not to take advantage of every change as much as possible. But many of the underlying factors remain the same. It would therefore be extremely foolish to assume otherwise. The use of foreign buzz-words does create some confusion, so it is best to check just what they mean and to what extent they truly exist. Not to do so would be more than merely foolish.

2
First Things First

Normally, a book – especially a how-to book – should start at the beginning. But that does not happen often with books on how to do business in Japan. They presume a lot of things. One is that every foreigner (*gaijin*) should be enthusiastic about cracking the Japanese market. But there are *gaijin* and *gaijin*. And what may be an excellent idea for some may be a rather poor one for others.

Yet, there you are on page 1, ready to negotiate your big deal with a Japanese company and the author hasn't even bothered telling you how you find a Japanese negotiating partner or how you determine which are the most likely candidates. Or, in other books, you are carefully designing your business card (*meishi*) which is to leave an indelible mark on the Japanese business world, and you don't even know if you should be going to Japan at all.

Well, I think you should start a bit earlier than that. You should begin with the essential, difficult and trying question of whether *you* (and not some fictionalized, standardized *gaijin*) should be doing business in Japan. This is a good idea for some companies. It is an absolutely lousy one for others. And you should not be printing your *meishi* until you come to a rational decision.

While not easy to make, that decision must have some appeal or it would not have attracted so many foreign companies (*gaishikei kigyo* or *gaishi* for short). Just how many is hard to know exactly. Still, according to recent trends, there must be about 3,500 foreign companies, the bulk of them American and European, established in Japan.[1] To this may be added hundreds more formed under Japanese law by foreigners living in Japan, thousands of companies licensing products, franchising services or transferring technologies and tens of thousands exporting one article or another.

Why did they come? That is what we will look at now.

Why go to Japan?

The general case for doing business in Japan is so well known, and inherently so convincing, that there is no need to belabor it. Thus, I will just highlight some of the more significant aspects. You can get much more in pep talks in the media or local chambers of commerce.

First of all, the Japanese market is large. It is very large. In fact, it is the second biggest in the world with Japan's consumer spending ranking second to the United States and per capita consumer spending, once converted into dollars, almost comparable. If you like round figures, you might mull over the fact that its gross national product is now about $5 trillion.

The market has grown this big, among other things, because Japan already has a population of some 125 million people, which is about half the size of the United States but more than twice that of larger European countries. They are crammed together in a relatively small space, only about as big as California, which makes the market exceptionally compact and easier to service in certain ways. The population is not increasing much nowadays, but the composition is shifting from many young to more old.

By the way, the Japanese are not just any people. They are people whose earnings have been growing steadily over the past decades, in fact even during the 1990s, if more slowly. They already have a per capita income which is higher than that of the United States and most of Europe. During this time, some of them were also enriched by astute real estate and stock market investments, although others have admittedly lost. And more and more are becoming richer because they are inheriting the wealth accumulated by hardworking elders.

The Japanese are known to be "frugal." That is a traditional virtue, and many still are, especially those hurt by the economic downturn of the 1990s. But others are quite rich, and flaunting that wealth, with all sorts of conspicuous consumption. During the 1990s, the savings rate remained high, as people were worried about the future and did not spend as readily. So there could just be another, equally "traditional" spending spree, once the economic situation improves. This means there is a very considerable pent-up demand which will eventually benefit companies prepared to receive it.

For such reasons the Japanese market is a very big market, still despite everything the second biggest, and it has a tendency to expand rapidly for another reason. The yen has undergone many ups and downs, certainly more ups than downs, as in the early 1990s. By the end of the 1990s, it was down again compared to the dollar and euro. However, since Japan is once again exporting itself out of a slump, the most likely future direction is up. The rise could easily be 25% or even twice that once the economy recovers. That would make the market far more attractive. And it would also make entering the market now, while the yen is relatively low, a smart strategy.

Of course, some sectors will be more interesting than others. In the past, Japan was mainly a place to sell fancy foreign luxury goods. That aspect will remain. But increasingly the Japanese are buying quite ordinary consumer goods, clothing, electronics, even automobiles, imported from many different sources, as long as they are cheaper. And there is still a demand for high-tech products and the technology to produce them. Meanwhile, with the shift in demographics toward more old people, there is a burgeoning market for anything sought by seniors, from health food to medicine. By far the biggest growth potential is in services, whether fast food, leisure, health care or financial.

Finally, the Japanese are under pressure to import more. For decades, the economy has been export-led, selling more than it bought. That sort of behavior naturally did not appeal to its trading partners which have pressured Japan to buy more from them. Since imports are presently at a comparatively low level, changing economic circumstances plus political pressure are opening the market like never before. This makes the present a considerably better time to do business in Japan than the past ever was.

But, should *you* go?

Fine, Japan is a great market! It did not take much to convince you. In fact, you probably already knew it. But this still doesn't answer the more pertinent question of whether this is a great market for you.

Such a question cannot be answered in the abstract. That much is obvious, although many foreigners try to crack the market without even bothering to consider it. For it is necessary at this point to dis-aggregate. You are not just any seller. You have a special product, of a specific quality, sold at a specific price, targeted at a specific segment, and so on. No matter what might be expected for any number of other products, you still have to ascertain whether yours will make the grade.

This implies that, as a first step, you should at least check on how your product will presumably fare. You have to see what the competing products are, if any. You have to see how yours compares. You have to determine whether the consumers are likely to be receptive. And you have to figure out the costs of marketing it so you know whether you can earn a reasonable return.

In so doing, you should remember that Japanese consumers may be considerably more demanding than your own. So, you must check whether the quality is good enough. You must be able to assure prompt and reliable delivery, otherwise Japanese distributors or manufacturers will not want to deal with you given their own imperatives. You must look into the aspect of service more closely, since the Japanese tend to be unusually fastidious about this. Further details are included in Chapter 9.

I'm certain you have heard all that before. The Japanese want quality, quality, quality, plus delivery, delivery, delivery, plus service, service, service. So do make an effort to provide that.

But don't forget about another aspect which most books on doing business in Japan overlook. That is price. Perhaps that is because so much emphasis is placed on quality, delivery, service, etc. But price is playing an increasingly important role. The first reason is very easy to understand. Because of the economic slowdown of the 1990s, many people feel less affluent than before and others are considerably worse off. Often they are stuck with heavy mortgage payments as well. This, increasingly large, category has to scrimp and save to get by. Thus, they are interested in bargains of all sorts, which they can find in cheaper shops or even, for the first time, second-hand outlets.

The second relates to a growing polarization of the population in terms of wealth. There are some truly "rich" people, or at least those who possess plenty of money which they tend to spend with unaccustomed abandon. They include those who have inherited substantial amounts, and also those who are just passing through a period when spending is the vogue. This includes especially young women (sometimes also men) who have a job but still live at home and can therefore spend nearly all their earnings on the good life. They are known as the "bachelor aristocrats" and they fuel many a consumer boom. At the other end are some who have become relatively (or absolutely) poorer. They often include, rather oddly, the parents of the "bachelor aristocrats" whose earnings have barely increased and, far worse off, the growing ranks of unemployed.[2]

This polarization has a far-reaching effect on the market. Many big ticket items (including automobiles) are postponed and the money is invested in smaller, more affordable pleasures like a meal out. Clothing is no longer quite as garish, and even fashionable young women splurge less. On the other hand, all sorts of electronics and photographic gear may be somewhat more ordinary. Things that are used around the house, where outsiders rarely appear, can be even more modest. The polarization can even border on schizophrenia with consumers spending more than they should on articles that are seen in public in order to maintain "face," while less is spent on the rest. This may imply spending more on luxuries and less on necessities, more on a Dior scarf and less on underwear, more on whiskey and less on tea.

Obviously, for many consumer articles and fashionable luxuries, price is almost no consideration. That means business is booming for Gucci, Dior and Remy Martin. This aspect is already well documented. Less known is that business is picking up notably for quite ordinary producers of quite ordinary articles. Many Korean, Taiwan, Hong Kong and other firms are now busily selling cheap watches, garments, household appliances, consumer electronics and so on. They are avidly sought by those in Japan who cannot afford anything else, a less notable but no less interesting clientele that should also keep growing.

By the way, I mentioned that you should check whether your product looks promising. I did not mean product in the restricted sense of a manufactured good. It could just as well be a service. The service sector is increasingly the most attractive for foreign companies. While the Japanese have done an excellent job of manufacturing, they have only been so-so when it comes to modern services.

For many, foreigners have more expertise and experience and could compete even more effectively than for manufactured goods.

So, check whether your product *or service* has what it takes to make it in Japan. But, even if it does not, you may still want to go. There is one last reason. And it may be the clincher.

With Japanese firms expanding aggressively overseas, whether through exports or investments, you will want to know what they are up to. You might do well to have a small office in Tokyo which would try to sell your product (or service) just to see how it fares. Meanwhile, it could also look into what your competitors are doing, whether they have come out with improved products or are expanding production. You may even get advance warning on how to react if the Japanese are preparing an export offensive. I think this is called a "listening post," but it could more correctly be assimilated to a spy operation.

Don't let them scare you off!

I would think that it is hard enough to make the decision of whether to go ahead without having to contend with all sorts of spurious reasons to hold back. There are ideas, arguments, rumors which are sometimes spread by quite reputable sources and intimate that, if one does not do something truly extraordinary, Japan is no place to be. I think they may be inspired by the Japanese, who don't want new competitors to begin with. Or they derive from the foreign mystique of how hard it is to do business in Japan. Whatever the case, they are unnecessary hindrances.

First of all, the notion that your product or service must be "unique" to succeed. Even the U.S. Department of Commerce foolishly insisted that retailers must be sure to offer "a unique product mix or service concept."[3] I never saw this mentioned in books on how to do business in America, or Europe, or China. Only for Japan is uniqueness a supposed requirement.

Well, how in this competitive world where everybody knows what everybody else is doing can you come up with "unique" products? Come to think of it, how many "unique" products are there around? How many products do something that no others do and are protected by patents or proprietary rights? And how many companies have access to such products?

If you look at what Japan imports, the bulk of it is hardly unique. Yes, there is a big place for brand name and high fashion articles, many high-tech products are sophisticated (if not quite unique), and there are patented pharmaceuticals, etc. But most of the stuff is quite ordinary, whether processed raw materials and foods, consumer articles, capital goods or services (banking, insurance, leisure, etc.). The further downmarket you go, the more ordinary it gets, with Taiwan's Tatung making a mint by selling electric fans!

No, even for Japan, you do not need something unique. But you should have something that is somewhat superior (or at least different). That can be in quality, design, convenience, service ... or price. You can sell the most ordinary of goods in the right sector if they are cheap enough. That is why exports from the nearby Asian countries, those which are stuck at the bottom of the market, are growing faster than those of more advanced countries which actually do have pretty special items.

So, the second mistaken reason not to try Japan is the concept that quality, delivery and service are all that count and if you cannot compare, forget Japan. They are important. They are terribly important. But they are not the only things that matter. You can be somewhat below par there and compensate with price. This means that comparative advantage, the same principle that governs trade everywhere else, also applies in Japan. Don't let them tell you otherwise!

Another must, according to the pundits, is commitment. You must be willing to put more up front in Japan, to wait for a longer time to penetrate the market, to wait yet longer to make a return on your investment, and to wait much more to be a true success. I don't disagree on the principle. But I question on details.

Obviously, you need commitment. Japan is a tough market. But that does not imply a massive effort. You can start off small and grow. That may be better than making too big a splash and finding you cannot meet your own expectations or those aroused in the marketplace. In addition, there are easier ways of entering, ones which require less commitment than a big wholly owned operation, such as a joint venture or merely exporting or licensing. For more on this, read Chapter 5.

(By the way, I am not even convinced that the commitment always has to be that exceptional. If you do your homework carefully, if you pick the right product or service, and market it in the right way, you may not have to wait so long for a decent return. Certainly not the eight years that are presently quoted as the necessary gestation period.)

Many foreigners feel that, since Japan has so many "big" companies, it is impossible to succeed if you are not "big". That is also a spurious worry. True, it does not hurt to be big, to have many products, lots of personnel and plenty of financial resources. But that is only decisive if your Japanese rivals are equally big or bigger. If you look more closely, you may find that your direct competitors are fairly small, maybe even smaller than you. In fact, there is an amazing number of small operations, often set up by a single foreigner (plus a Japanese spouse in some cases), that made a go of it. There are also countless small companies that discovered just the right niche and are prospering.[4]

One other misconception, which is never openly expressed, is racial. Virtually all of the literature on doing business in Japan implicitly assumes that the companies are Western. After all, you want a unique product, you need great experience, you require enormous financial clout and it is good if you are in high tech. Who meets those qualifications? The big Western multinationals. But, as noted, there is ever more room in other sectors which make none of these demands and where price is an essential factor. That surely signifies that there is room for companies from developing countries, especially the nearby Asian "newly industrialized countries."

Finally, sexual discrimination ... in the literature and in Japan. True, the Japanese do not think very highly of the business acumen of women. Indeed, if they suspected a businesswoman were competent, it might repel them more than attract them. Foreign businessmen also seem to think that only a tough macho approach will work. Still, many foreign women have managed to set up and run their own companies, although they rarely appear on the staffs of the foreign multinationals. Be that as it may, they face more hurdles than men and, in practice, most of the participants in the business world are men, especially on the Japanese side.

Still tough, but less so

The purpose of this chapter is not to talk you into doing business but to explain, as well as I can, what the advantages and drawbacks are. While indicating that many obstacles are not as serious or valid as thought, I would not like to imply that Japan is an easy market. It is not. It is a tough market. It is damn tough.

First of all, you have to face competition which is more intense than what you are familiar with back home, no matter where that may be. Japanese companies compete with one another more aggressively than do American, or German, or even Korean companies. That is because much of the competition is based on market share, a much harsher task master than mere profit.

Liberal market economies have a win–win ethos. You try to boost profits by increasing the margin, something which does not necessarily upset your competitors. In fact, it allows them to raise margins and boost profits as well. Admittedly, in hard times there is pressure, and you would bring down prices, obliging others to do the same. But you would not want to lower them so far as to endanger profits under ordinary circumstances. Price-cutting and competitive wars are more the exception.

In Japan, they are almost the rule because you must undercut your competitors to increase market share. This is a very serious matter since now you are in a win–lose situation. If you gain market share, somebody must lose, because there is only 100%. This leaves foreign companies in a bind when competing with Japanese rivals, for they would not want to lower prices enough to hurt the bottom line. Yet, if they do not fight back, they will gradually lose market share no matter how fine profits are. The end result could be that they are driven out of the market.

In addition, you will be coping with unusually demanding customers. These may be ordinary consumers, men and women who want the best in quality, service, etc. and will be almost fastidious in their selection. You will not get off any easier if you sell to Japanese companies. They are strict in their demands of quality, delivery, service and price. You have probably already heard this before, so there is no need to expand on it now.

These are "natural" barriers, in the sense of arising spontaneously in the market and not being man-made. There are also lots of artificial barriers blocking access to Japan. No matter how often or how earnestly Japanese politicians, bureaucrats and businessmen insist that Japan is one of the world's most open markets, that is not quite true. The Japanese have demonstrated great ingenuity in devising obstacles to keep out imported goods. To learn more about them, you should read *Unlocking Japan's Markets*.[5]

The good thing is that these barriers are decreasing. Tariff levels have declined considerably. Indeed, by now the average rate is lower than in most industrialized countries, although you may encounter peaks in certain sectors. Quotas are disappearing aside from some foodstuffs and leather goods. Nontariff barriers do remain. The Japanese have eliminated hundreds of NTBs, but they did not get rid of all of them. Moreover, when nobody is looking, they try to create new ones. Still, even these are not insurmountable.

What does pose a serious problem even now are the tight relations that exist between Japanese companies. This can be the reputed warm and friendly relations that derive from cooperating with one another for decades. Or it can involve harder, more resistant links resulting from financial control, shareholding, domination of retailing, etc. This is typified by the groups or *keiretsu* which will be dealt with in more detail in the next chapter.

Fortunately, no matter how irritating or inhibiting, these assorted barriers are – on the whole – receding and it is getting easier to penetrate the market. Not only that the Japanese government has been shamed into actually promoting imports. It has taken various steps which redound to the advantage of foreign companies. Among other things, it urges Japanese manufacturers to procure more parts or equipment abroad, it suggests that individual consumers buy more imported goods, and it organizes special "buy foreign" campaigns. In addition, specialized bodies promote import missions and trade fairs and undertake other activities to help foreigners enter the market. Certainly, this effort has been less fruitful than the earlier export drives, but it has created a much more congenial environment.

Still, don't expect the Japanese to take you by the hand (unless they have to meet their "quota" of imported goods). If you want to make it in Japan, you must do the right things in the right ways. You have to figure out how to get around the barriers and live with the business structure and cultural hangups. This will be discussed in subsequent chapters.

What to do before you go

Once you have decided to tackle the Japanese market, you should prepare. Obviously according to all the manuals, the first thing to do is print up some *meishi*. These are the Japanese version of business cards which are distributed profusely and you may well need hundreds. They should be bilingual, your language plus Japanese. That is, assuming your language is an alphabet or character one readily grasped by the Japanese. Otherwise, and even for some European languages, perhaps English would be the better second language.

Meishi can often be made in your home country by local translation companies or major airlines, especially Japanese carriers. But just hope and pray that the translation is correct. Otherwise you may end up a laughing stock. Just in case, bring along some of your old cards. The alternative is to have them made in Japan. The turnaround is fast, the price is high, but there is still no guarantee of quality. Not even in Japan!

As all intelligent businessmen should realize, you don't just plunk your *meishi* on the table. You hand it formally to your counterparts, making a bow of 15°. You collect theirs and inspect them earnestly. You do not dump them unceremoniously in your pocket or deal them out like a deck of cards on the table. What's that? How do you know your bow is the regulation 15°. Academics are so remiss in details of this nature. I assume you can draw a line on your office wall and practice every day.

You should also get a foretaste of Japan and things Japanese, according to certain authors. Yes, why not go out for a good Japanese dinner? Try the *sushi*, it provides excellent practice to learn the art of wielding chopsticks and is served at most receptions. You may not like the octopus, but that can be forgiven a *gaijin*. Also get in some drinking practice. It is amazing how much useful information can be obtained over a glass of whisky. No, tipping is not necessary. And, even if the waiter bows to you, you should not bow back. Save that for your hosts.

You might also acquaint yourself with Japanese culture. Attend a Kabuki or Noh presentation, if there is one around. Or get a video of Kurosawa's *Seven Samurai*. Since you are a businessman, you may be tempted to read more books on doing business in Japan. That should not hurt, at least not too much. It all depends on how informative or misleading they are, with the latter outnumbering the former by at least two or three to one. That is why I am suggesting some good ones here and there in the text and in the footnotes. But steer clear of those which make Japanese business appear overly exotic or trace success back to Samurai virtues or Zen.

Admittedly, there are other things you could do as well. I have rarely seen them referred to in the basic primers, so I can only assume that other authors regard them as less important. I personally think they are crucial.

For example, you might contact the nearest office of the Japan External Trade Organizations. JETRO, as it is known, has over forty offices overseas in about twenty countries. They are amply staffed with experienced officials who know the Japanese market and can help you develop a feel for it. JETRO offers a broad range of publications, including more general ones on how the economy works, how to use the distribution system, how to establish joint ventures and how to market specific products. The *JETRO Marketing Series* covers the basics, and *Your Market in Japan* has individual reports on a multitude of product lines. Further useful literature is available in the library.[6] JETRO will not find you a partner, but it can suggest where to look for one. And its *Japan Trade Directory* has useful data on several thousand Japanese companies and associations foreigners may wish to contact. This way you could write ahead.

Indeed, you may not even have to wait for an answer. After all, numerous Japanese companies have offices abroad, especially in countries with which they do more business. This includes the general trading companies, and also specialized trading companies, as well as major manufacturers and retailers, and of course the banks and securities companies. You can find their addresses in JETRO's *Directory of Japanese Affiliated Companies in the USA and Canada* or the *Directory of Japanese Affiliated Companies in Asia* or in the *Yellow Pages Japan in USA (and Canada)*.

Over in Japan, you may wish to visit JETRO again. It has a huge office in Tokyo, with abundant staff and an enormous library, and smaller offices in two dozen other cities. It also has "Import Squares," "Antenna Shops," exhibition halls and Import Information Centers in such locations as Tokyo, Osaka, Kobe, Nagoya and Yokohama. Another helpful body is the Manufactured Imports Promotion Organization (MIPRO) in Tokyo which helps out for sales of manufactures with advice, information, working space and exhibition halls. Members of the Association of Southeast Asian Nations should certainly visit, and perhaps work through, the ASEAN Centre in Tokyo. Newcomers of whatever nationality may also wish to display their wares in one of JETRO's Import Fairs or the literally hundreds of other specialized fairs, exhibitions and trade shows that are organized every year for specific branches.[7]

But do not assume that Tokyo, or the other larger cities, are all that exist in Japan. Interesting possibilities can also be found in the prefectures. Some of these have opened "local internationalization centers" which advise on market entry and supply temporary space. Of particular note are some two dozen Foreign Access Zones, which were established under a special law to promote imports and foreign investment. The FAZs are located next to ports and airports and provide essential services like bonded warehouses, processing, refrigeration and fumigation facilities, joint distribution centers, joint wholesale facilities and so on. Firms operating there are eligible for special tax benefits and preferential financing. Information on the FAZs can also be obtained through JETRO.

By now, most foreign embassies in Tokyo can also provide information and some backup through the commercial section. Some countries go further and assist nationals back home through the Ministry of Trade, Department of Commerce, or special trade offices similar to JETRO like HKTDC in Hong Kong and KOTRA in Korea. The United States International Trade Administration has been making a concerted effort through various programs including the Japan Export and Information Program, the Trade Promotion Cooperation Program and the Japan Export Promotion Program. They offer information and advice on entry strategies, standards and testing, restrictions and barriers, and market research. They also pinpoint special opportunities.

While not as entertaining as movies or pop culture, there are some very dull books you might consider which can help you find partners and, equally important, know who your major competitors are. You can look up the listed ones in Toyo Keizai's *Japan Company Handbook*. You can find out how strong they are in *Market Share in Japan* published annually by Yano Research Institute. You may get leads from JETRO's *Market Guidebook for Major Imported Products*. And you can see how companies were interlinked through Dodwell's *Industrial Groupings in Japan*.

What you should be doing, when you are not busy eating *sushi* or practicing bowing, is scrutinizing these and other publications. Before setting foot in Japan, you should know something about the market for your product, who else sells the same line, how the various rivals stack up, who their major shareholders are and what their turnover and profits look like. That may not be culture in the ordinary sense, but it is the best way of making your visit a success.

One last tip. You might reflect on *how* to go. It is not wise just to fly out to Japan without any appointments or introductions. You cannot simply cold call or knock on doors. Your hosts must be fore-warned. That can be done, not terribly well but better than nothing, by writing to those you have singled out. The commercial section of your embassy may be able to help. So can some of the foreign chambers of commerce in Japan. I would strongly recommend contacting the embassy and the chamber well in advance to see what they can do to prepare your trip.

A very interesting alternative is to join a trade mission organized by the U.S. Department of Commerce, Hong Kong Trade Development Council, or whatever national entity is in charge of such things. It will take care of most of the petty and bothersome logistics, like travel, hotels, secretarial and interpreting services, etc. It will also try to attract as many potential Japanese customers or partners as possible. You can then make contacts and perhaps conclude some deals, although that usually takes longer. If you are wise, you can use this as a springboard for a longer stay.

Another springboard is the trade shows or exhibitions, of which there are hundreds, each concentrating on a specific sector. Attend one that covers your line. It is the easiest way of getting broad exposure, meeting potential customers and partners, and also seeing what the competition is offering. Again, the event's organizer may be helpful with accommodations, services, etc. You could extend your stay to follow up on useful contacts.

With this kind of preparation and this kind of introduction, your progress should be much faster and more fruitful than otherwise. To get more details, contact the appropriate national or state office, the relevant trade association or JETRO, the embassy and chamber of commerce. They are there to help you. And don't forget to take along a bunch of gifts to thank everyone who has been helpful. As we all know, the Japanese are great gift givers (and receivers).

3
Corporate Community

Of course, you are going to *Japan* to do business. But Japan is a big place and, no matter how big you are, you will really only be doing business in some small corner of that vast market. So, the sooner the better, you must begin disaggregating and figuring out just what sort of business community you will fit into. Like anywhere else, you must know the players and how they operate. Only then can you decide how best to react.

Unfortunately, most foreign businessmen arrive in Japan and assume either that it is just like back home, with some minor variations, or that it is completely different. Neither extreme is right. But the structure you encounter is more likely to be different than the same. And you will avoid many painful mistakes if you realize that from the outset. The only country in the world with a similar structure is South Korea. Germany comes closest among the Western economies, but even it is considerably more loose and liberal. Comparisons with a free-wheeling place like the United States will probably be wrong.

There are various reasons for this. One, which will be dealt with next, is that companies are organized differently and have some different goals and functions. The very employment system differs. Companies are also much more closely linked, often forming groups not only of allies and associates but potential competitors. If you don't know how they operate and how they cooperate, you are in for many surprises. The following is an effort to clarify the situation enough for you to work out your own position in Japan's corporate community. With luck, it will make your foreign firm a bit less alien.

Companies large and small

Foreigners who have never visited Japan, and many who have spent some time there, tend to assume that it is the realm of huge corporations, corporations with immense human and financial resources, offices around the world, and incredible commercial clout. That is not surprising. After all, that is the only kind of company most *gaijin* are exposed to. No matter where we live, we are already familiar with such giants as Mitsui and Mitsubishi, Toyota and Nissan, Bank of Tokyo and Industrial Bank of Japan, Nomura and Daiwa, Matsushita and Hitachi, and many more.

A closer look shows something quite different. These big companies (*dai kigyo*), the ones we know so well, only account for about 1% of all Japanese companies. Admittedly, they employ about 30% of all workers and control a larger amount of assets, sales and so on. But, even considering their size, they remain a minority. The rest are classified as small and medium enterprises (*chu-sho kigyo*) which together amount to 99% of all companies with 70% of the labor force. This juxtaposition of big and small generates what is frequently called a "dual structure."

To some extent, the big companies and smaller ones are in different sectors. The overwhelming majority of the smaller enterprises are in construction, distribution (mom-and-pop stores) or services (fast food, personal and business services, leisure). But many are in manufacturing, frequently in more backward areas but sometimes in quite advanced ones. Often the big and small share a sector, the big banks and the small consumer loan firms, the big automakers and the small parts suppliers, the big steel mills and the small fabricators. To understand Japan, it is indispensable to consider both.

To function in Japan, it is necessary to deal with both and remember that they often operate on a different basis. For example, big companies recruit the best students from the best schools; small ones get what is left over. Big companies offer "lifetime employment," at least to the extent it exists. Small companies tend to hire and fire more readily. Employees of big companies earn more, work less and enjoy better conditions than employees of small companies. We shall see what this means to the Japanese and to foreigners doing business in Japan further on.

A more decisive aspect of the duality is that smaller companies are often dependent on or at least beholden to larger companies. In distribution, small stores and shops frequently sell the produce of the large companies. Small service firms curry to their needs. Small factories busily turn out parts and components that big companies assemble into finished products. But they rarely do so as free agents. There is one link or another which establishes a fairly rigid, hierarchical relationship. That is the key to so much of what happens in Japan that a foreigner will never know his way around without studying these relationships.

Groups and *keiretsu*

In Japan, it is not enough to know the players as such, it is essential to know with which other companies they have close relations of one sort or another. Only then can you evaluate their true strength and potential and decide whether to work with or avoid them. That is because links are so prevalent and so important. Virtually every company is tied to many others in various ways which reinforce or restrict its action. Frequently, these links are highly structured and form a clearly definable circle of associates or a full-fledged group.[1]

There are three basic types of links or "alignments" you should watch for since they fashion the three basic types of groups or *keiretsu*. One is a circle of large companies which revolves around a bank and is thus called a bank or capital group. The second is a coterie of smaller suppliers and subcontractors organized by a large manufacturer which is known as an enterprise group. The third consists of captive outlets of major producers, the distribution group.

Most familiar is the bank group or *kin'yu keiretsu* which in some cases grew out of the earlier *zaibatsu* and in others resulted from efforts of rising banks to emulate them. This alignment brings together major players in just about every important sector, not only a bank but a trading company, insurers, assorted manufacturers and some service establishments. These companies are relatively independent and equal members which cooperate in their mutual interest, either to do business with one another or launch joint projects. You will recognize the names of leading ones like Mitsui, Mitsubishi, Sumitomo, Fuyo (Fuji), Dai-Ichi Kangyo, Sanwa, etc. (See Figure 3.1.)

Figure 3.1 The Sumitomo Group

Source: Dodwell Marketing Consultants, *Industrial Groupings in Japan, 1991,* p. 78.

The enterprise group (*kigyo keiretsu*) is basically a network of suppliers and subcontractors for manufacturers and thus looks rather familiar. But it is a much tighter unit than elsewhere, since the suppliers are much more dependent on the manufacturer, to the extent where their operations are partly integrated in its own. There is also a greater tendency to buy only within this network and not go outside even if cheaper supplies could be obtained. Such groups can be found in many sectors: autos, ships, steel, chemicals, electronics. Familiar names are Toyota and Nissan, Nippon Steel, Asabi Chemical, Hitachi, Toshiba, Sony and so on. (See Figure 3.2.)

The distribution groups (*ryutsu keiretsu*) involve distributors for many consumer goods, from automobiles to household appliances, from watches to eyeglasses, including also cosmetics and electronics. The wholesalers and retailers are again more dependent than elsewhere. They are also particularly numerous, running into the thousands and even tens of thousands. More decisive, captive outlets may account for the majority of all outlets with even supposedly "independent" ones restricted to several Japanese makes. There is no need to name names, any producer in the sector must have its own network if it is to prosper.

While the three categories can be distinguished conceptually, it is worthwhile noting that many leading companies belong to more than one. Manufacturers are often part of a bank *keiretsu*: they have their own subcontracting network and sell through a circle of related distributors. The best examples are the automakers and electronics firms. This makes the "big" Japanese companies much bigger than they appear at first sight. For what it is worth, it also makes the "small" enterprises weaker and more dependent.

There is a tendency to tell gullible foreigners that these groups are just the result of Japanese preferences for stable, long-term relations. That sounds good, reasonable and irreproachable. But the realities are quite different. Links are based not on affinity but material control through share crossholding in bank groups and financial domination of suppliers and retailers through shareholding, loans and advances. Large companies also appoint key personnel in smaller ones or impose on them by being the sole supplier or buyer.

Why this interest in *keiretsu*? Because they are major pillars of the Japanese business community? Because you will encounter them everywhere you turn? Because you must adjust to them? Yes. That.

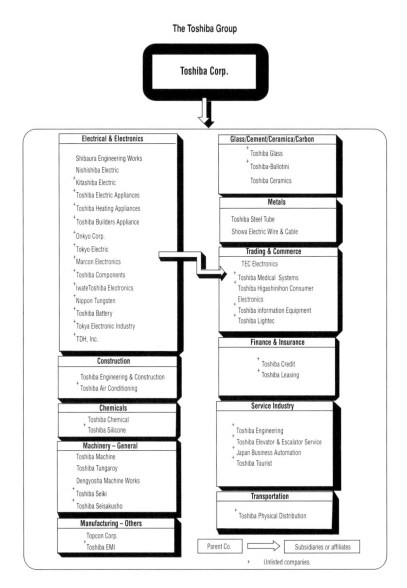

Figure 3.2   The Toshiba Group

Source: Dodwell Marketing Consultants, *Industrial Groupings in Japan, 1991*, p. 217.

And one thing more. The *keiretsu* are an immense market in themselves. The eight largest account for nearly a fifth of Japan's turnover. They also do a lot of business amongst themselves, about 13% of intergroup transactions for the looser bank groups and as much as 30–50% for the enterprise groups.[2] This means that if you can tie up with a *keiretsu*, you may have privileged access to major clients. On the other hand, you may have trouble dealing with companies in other groups.

Business organizations

The Japanese are also big believers in business organizations. Most of them appear rather familiar. You have something like that, or at least called by the same name, in your own country. But they often possess greater prerogatives and prestige in Japan. You should seriously consider whether to join, not for social but business reasons. You may not. You may wish to stay aloof. But you can be certain that they are still aware of your presence.

Particularly interesting are the trade associations.[3] They exist for just about every conceivable sector. Some sprang up spontaneously, others were instigated by the government because the establishment feels that the existence of such organizations makes for a stabler, stronger economy. Sometimes the sectors are quite narrow so that larger foreign companies may fall under the purview of several.

These trade associations bring together all the major players and some of the minor ones but not every last firm. Together with officials in the relevant ministry, they work out regulations that should apply to their activities. Companies also cooperate to define technical standards. While not strictly legitimate, they tend to be somewhat restrictive in that they do not readily accept newcomers and foreigners, alas, are often newcomers. *Gaishi* are also harder to assimilate. To join, and there are definite advantages, foreign companies must show they can conform to the rules and are sometimes supervised until they become fully accepted.

Even when not overly hospitable, contacts with the trade association can be extremely useful. For one, it is possible to learn which companies do what and which might eventually become partners or associates. One can get a better idea of how the sector is regulated and policed. The trade association is keenly aware of what the government is planning and it usually plays a crucial role in shaping new legislation and regulations.

The Japan Chamber of Commerce and Industry, and the local chambers, are not only more familiar, they tend to function more like their counterparts abroad. Given the clannishness of Japanese companies and the difficulty in meeting their executives more informally, this can be an excellent entrée. It is also much easier for *gaijin* to join. But do not expect to achieve too much concretely.

The real source of power in the business community is the Japan Federation of Economic Organizations or Keidanren, which brings together the largest companies in an extremely influential forum. Similar bodies abroad are a mere shadow of it. Keidanren not only advises the political leaders, it funds them. It not only discusses problems with senior bureaucrats, it usually imposes its line on them. But until recently it was an exclusively Japanese club. Now it is finally opening up to foreign companies.

Where the *gaishi* can go, and most definitely should go, is the foreign chamber of commerce if one exists for your country. There is an American, Canadian, French, German and Italian chamber as well as one for Australia and New Zealand.[4] There are similar forums for some other nationalities. These bodies are a source of information, a place to meet counterparts and learn from more experienced Japan hands, and a good starting point in seeking partners and associates or consultants and lawyers. The chambers also try to influence the Japanese government with regard to foreign interests.

Japan is no place for loners, whether individuals or companies. More than elsewhere, it is necessary to belong. And what you belong to can make a very big difference in your future success.

Government relations

Many foreign businessmen, especially Western ones, do not think much of the government's role. They come from countries where it is relatively minor and companies are free to conduct their affairs as they like, within the limits of the law. There is not much to be gained from currying favor with government leaders or even listening to what they have to say. They would be foolish to assume that they can go about their business as freely in Japan.

In Japan, government does matter. It matters very much. It does considerably more than just lay down a broad framework in which business can be conducted. It often works out rather minute procedures which must be followed. These procedures, by the way, may not even be written or exist in a sense. They are provided not only by laws, regulations and the like but "administrative guidance" (*gyosei shido*). This is advice, formulated case-by-case for specific circumstances and which may well not be repeated even in similar circumstances. The only way to obtain it is to ask specifically, and violating such unwritten rules, even if they are not known, would be most impolitic.[5]

Admittedly, when I speak of the government's role, I am not thinking of the role of the politicians. They may be uppermost in Western and developing societies; in Japan, it is the bureaucrats who call the shots. It is therefore necessary to get to know the bureaucrats in your sector. This means officials of the Finance Ministry for banks, insurance and securities firms, Ministry of International Trade and Industry for manufacturers, Ministry of Health for pharmaceuticals, etc.

These officials can inform you about the various intricate regulations existing for imports. They can give you pointers on how to – and not to – conduct business in your line. They grant all sorts of permits and authorizations ... or not, depending on what they think of you. Of course, you will not be able to deal with senior officials at the outset. You will have to make do with quite junior personnel who should be treated with great respect not because of their ability but their position and what they can do to help or hinder your efforts. Anyway, with time, they will rise and become more influential.

While most rules and regulations are neutral and apply equally to everyone, you are bound to encounter some which appear biased against your company or foreigners in general. There used to be thousands of them. Now there may just be hundreds. For the ministries have been severely criticized by foreign governments and endeavor to appear more enlightened. Be that as it may, you may well run into a remaining nontariff barrier or superfluous regulation whose compliance demands costly and time-consuming efforts.

If a regulation works against you, something must be done other than allowing it to stymie your progress. That something can be a complaint to your embassy, which may or may not wish to help out. If it does, it may influence the bureaucracy in your favor. It may also get their backs up. So the first effort should probably be a gentle, diplomatic one with a rcsort to official rccourse only later. By the way, the Japanese government has appointed an ombuds-man to look into grievances. Unfortunately, so far he has been neither quick nor effective.

Where do you fit in?

The above information was not provided to expand your cultural outlook or emphasize just how different those Japanese are. The purpose was to describe the lay of the land so that when you move in you have a better idea of what to expect. The new guy on the block should always be aware of who is around and who really counts. He should know his neighborhood and try to fit in. Fitting in is particularly important in Japan because the Japanese expect the newcomers to adapt as smoothly as possible and without creating too much fuss and bother for the old-timers.

For one, you might remember that size matters in Japan. How big you are counts almost as much as who you are in a dual structure where the big and small behave quite differently and interrelate in specific ways. You should realize that your own behavior should differ if you are a large, prestigious foreign firm or a tiny, inconse-quential one. Forget any notions of all being equal or making up for size with imagination and drive. That is not the prevailing ethos and – on the surface at least – knowing your place is useful.

By the way, in this polarized arena of very large and very small, you may discover that you are not as small as you thought. You may still be considerably larger than your counterparts in certain sectors or certain activities where small firms are prevalent, such as services and distribution. On the other hand, even if you are quite big back home, once you consider the group relationships of your potential partners or competitors, you may discover that they are bigger than you thought.

Big and small is just the start. There is a definite tendency for the former to dominate the latter. Relations are much more structured and equality is not even a theoretical goal. In particular, suppliers and subcontractors should expect stiffer conditions than back home. They will also have less leverage and less chance to work with a broad array of customers. If you cannot accept such relations, if you cannot comply with such conditions, there is not much point to looking for business in Japan.

On the other hand, if you happen to be buying goods from Japanese suppliers, you can expect them to go that extra mile. They will go out of their way to satisfy whatever conditions you may lay down. They will find it quite normal that the conditions are strict. Indeed, if you are too lax or lenient, they are quite likely to lose respect for your company. You should know where you fit in not only when you are below but when you are on top.

In a business community in which local companies have multiple relations with other companies, especially associates, it is hard to go it alone. This may be your philosophy back home. It would be wise to modify it in Japan. Even if you can produce your own parts, sell your own goods, finance your own needs, it is extremely useful just to make friends who can do the same thing for you. In some cases, they cannot do it any better; in others, they can. However, the simple fact of doing business with you will increase their interest in your succeeding and they may help out in ways you would not expect.

In Japan, competition is fierce. It is often nastier than abroad. Yet, even competitors know how to cooperate in their mutual interest. This can be done through the trade associations or more informal gatherings. It can be done by adjusting relations with other sectors or the government. But so much is going on that a mere bystander will miss it. Participating is more purposeful. It will not make you an insider, certainly not quickly. But it will at least make your *gaishi* less of an outsider in a society that does not really like outsiders.

Given the prevalence of groups, and the tight and chummy relations between group members, it would be smart always to check on who associates with whom. This should apply to your competitors, since you want to know just how strong they are. You want to know who their bankers are, who their suppliers are, who distributes their goods and so on. You also want to know how strong any links are and what they imply for you. That much is obvious.

Less obvious is that you must scrutinize potential partners more than elsewhere. You must find out who their associates are, their bankers, suppliers, distributors, etc. That way you will know just how strong they are, how much they can contribute to any joint effort. You can also discover just now eager they are to contribute. After all, it is possible that even if the prospective partner is not a direct competitor, it may have associates within the broader *keiretsu* who are. And this could crimp its style.

If you can adopt this approach in dealing with Japanese companies, your chances of success will be immeasurably greater. For that is how they operate. They do not think solely of their own interests or the relationship with your company but how this all affects the broader business community. That was clearly stated by Mark Zimmerman, former president of the American Chamber of Commerce in Japan and head of several joint ventures:

> The questions revolving in the mind of a Japanese contemplating a deal are how the industrial group with which he is affiliated will view the new arrangement with a foreign company; what the association of his industry will have to say; and whether he will be taking unfair advantage, thus causing his competitors to react violently. In fact, the Japanese is as concerned with the impact of the agreement on his standing within the Japanese business community as he is with direct monetary benefits that his firm will derive from the arrangements.[6]

More homework before you go

I hate to be so demanding, but before you leave for Japan, it would be exceedingly useful to do some more homework.

This time you should do very careful research on your sector in order to determine whether it is dominated by a few large companies or spread among many small ones, so you know whether you stand a chance of squeezing in. You may get some insight into that through the documentation of the trade association or at least the membership list. *Market Share in Japan* will let you know which ones are on top. Further information can be obtained from JETRO, the embassy or local business consultants.

Even more important, you should check on your potential partners and competitors. This time it is not a question of what their products are, what they cost, how they compare. It is more a matter of determining who they are related to for the reasons just mentioned. You do not want to find out that your competitors are stronger than you thought, that your prospective partner is weaker or that it is hampered by relations with other companies.

It is not easy to trace all the links. But the Dodwell publications certainly point you in the right direction. *Industrial Groupings in Japan* indicates the membership of the largest groups with lists not only of the members but many of their own subsidiaries and affiliates. Insight into enterprise groups is provided in the volumes on the electronics and automobile industries. You will have a fairly good idea of what is supplied within the "family," what possible gaps may exist and who you will have to compete with if you want the business.

Naturally, such literature only covers the major sectors and companies. It also only has so much information. To fill in the gaps, it may be necessary to have more exhaustive studies run by appropriate bodies. Your embassy or foreign chamber of commerce can probably provide names of reliable companies specialized in this sort of research.

*   *   *

This is the last time I will suggest specific homework since you should have more than enough to keep you busy once you arrive in Japan. However, I would recommend further reading. Obviously, each of these chapters is much too small to go into detail on all aspects and some excellent books (as well as some pretty mediocre ones) are available to fill in with additional information. I would strongly urge you to read some of them and therefore list more useful books or publications in the footnotes. They are presented in full, with publisher, in the bibliography.

4
Business-Related Culture

Somewhere along the line, most books on doing business in Japan lapse into fanciful reflections on Japanese culture. They muse about the ancient customs and traditions, how the Japanese personality is forged by mutual obligation (*giri* and *on*) or the time-honored loyalty of the *samurai* toward his lord. They explain how flower arrangement or tea ceremony or goodness knows what shapes the inner workings of the Japanese mind. Foreigners must be very sensitive and subtle in adjusting to these cultural factors if they are to succeed in the business world, it is argued.

No! Well, yes and no. There is not the slightest doubt that culture has a deep and pervasive influence on the Japanese, like everybody else, and that cultural factors must be considered. But they tend to pick the wrong factors and impute rather exotic and far-fetched consequences. Most of today's Japanese, the living, breathing ones you are likely to meet, are affected by very different conditions and impulses. They are much more real and much more effective. And, if you miss them, you could do quite poorly in trying both to comprehend Japan and make some money there.

After all, aside from the older business and government leaders (many already in semi-retirement), most company executives, ministry officials, workers and consumers are heirs to a very different culture. One that is more open, one that is more affluent and one that has forgotten so many of the ancient and honorable ways that their parents and grandparents wonder just how Japanese they are. In fact, when Japanese companies send their employees off to a foreign posting nowadays, they have to first be taught what

"Japanese culture" is all about so as to answer questions from inquisitive foreigners.

Lifetime employment

One of the practical manifestations you are bound to encounter is what is loosely called "lifetime employment." This embodies not only a different form of recruitment, promotion, remuneration and so on, it creates a different work world. It is extremely important to understand what the implications are for the Japanese – and also the foreign businessman – if ever you are to establish your own company here or even use the services of a local one. But forget about quaint notions of the company family, the caring employer, the loyal worker and the like. The explanations are cruder and more forceful.

As a start, of course, you should realize that lifetime employment does not exist in all companies. It takes a rather large one to recruit enough personnel to make the system meaningful. It therefore prevails in the upper tier (actually perhaps 10%) of the companies by number with perhaps 40% of the total work force. The rest, smaller and even medium-sized firms, just emulate it in some way or merely pay lip-service. Even where it exists, it most emphatically does not include women, part-time or temporary workers or those who joined the company part-way through their career. So, at best 15–20% of the total labor force is included.

A further point. It is not "lifetime." The system covers employees from entry until the official retirement age, which varies from company to company is now about 57. Most still have to work until the age of 60, 65 and more to get by.

Other employees are dropped even before reaching retirement. We are told that dismissal *only* occurs in exceptional circumstances and for grievous misbehavior. Maybe so. Alas, companies also shed staff by transferring them to suppliers and subcontractors, by setting up small firms to absorb them or just suggesting that they would be wise to retire now with a bonus rather than hang around.

How does the system work … for those lucky enough to enjoy it? That cannot be entirely summarized in the following, and much more background can be found in *Japan's Wasted Workers* and other books listed in the bibliography.[1] Still, some salient features convey the essence.

First of all, youngsters are recruited directly from school, whether a high school, vocational school or college. They have no previous experience and, in case you are interested, their employers like it that way. They want to form young, impressionable workers in their own manner and turn them into loyal employees. That explains why so much emphasis is placed on education, or rather, graduating from the right schools since major companies tend to recruit from the same sources. This is done year after year and each year a large, relatively undifferentiated crop of young school leavers is harvested.

These new employees are distributed among the various offices and plants and trained on the job. There may be some formal training, but not all that much. The rest comes from watching what older workers do and being integrated in the team. Most will stay in a given posting for two or three years and then rotate to another, regularly at this rhythm, getting to know the company and its personnel extremely well. Those on the fast track will *not* specialize. They remain generalists. Specialists, engineers, mechanics, designers, bookkeepers and the like will be stuck in the same place much longer and rarely reach the top.

As employees are rotated, they also rise gradually. They move up with the "career escalator," from year to year, with a steadily rising salary and increasingly more impressive title. What they do in each assignment, how capable they are, how dedicated they are, how hard working and long suffering they are will make relatively little difference during most of the ride. Seniority is the rule. The big difference comes when the few are selected to become executives and the many are sent off to subsidiaries or suppliers or asked to retire gracefully.

However, before thinking how nice it is … at least for those who reach the top, let me interject that there is not just one escalator. There are several. One is for male college graduates, which starts part way up and goes from modest white-collar positions to company president sometimes. There is another for male high school graduates, which allocates blue-collar jobs that may eventually lead to a supervisory post in the factory. The third and fourth are for women, with high school graduates sent to the assembly lines and college graduates entering the offices, but with less responsibility and chance of promotion. For them, "lifetime" employment is rather short, just a few years until they get married, have children or become a bore.

Worse, many female employees are very poorly used even while they are around. This applies much less to the factory workers than the white- or pink-collar employees. They are given rather little incentive to perform well and even less initiative. Indeed, many are relegated to humdrum tasks like running errands, taking phone calls and typing letters. That is, when they are not busy ushering in customers or serving tea. They are given the informal title of "office lady" or OL. But it is a frightful waste of time and talent.

When you do business with the Japanese, you will meet almost exclusively "lifetime employees," from the president down to the girl serving tea. These are company men (or women) who are probably more devoted to their company's success than you are to that of your own. Don't forget that. It is not a question of cooperation, or harmonious relations or give-and-take, they were sent to win and the personal commitment and urge to win is much greater. On the other hand, if doing business with you will enhance their chances of winning (especially against other Japanese companies), they can be very stalwart – if not entirely trustworthy – allies.

That is just one of the consequences of this modern Japanese business culture. There are many others, some of which will be discussed in the following sections. So, put aside your copy of *The Chrysanthemum and the Sword* or *The Book of Five Rings* and consider some realities.

Company loyalty

Enthusiastic commentators compare today's "salaryman," the ubiquitous, all-purpose white-collar employee with yesteryear's *samurai*. Certainly, the *sarariman* is devoted to his company, dependent on his company and willing to sacrifice his time and even personal life for his company. He will stay with his company through thick and thin until the "lifetime" stint is over. But that has less to do with *giri* and obligation than with other, more compelling factors.

Company employees are loyal because of the lifetime employment system. First of all, they are recruited directly from school and have no previous experience of another company, so they can hardly compare employers. In addition, few are specialized enough to offer specific skills to any other employer. All they know, and that they know exceedingly well, is how their own company operates and who does what. But that is hardly transferable. Nobody else would hire them just for that.

Given the cult of loyalty throughout corporate Japan, few other large companies would want to hire them if they left their earlier employer even if they did have special skills. True, there has been some job hopping of late. But most companies do not like "traitors" or find it easy to integrate anyone who joins them in mid-career or, indeed, anywhere but the bottom of the escalator. Added to this, of course, there is an unwritten no-poaching rule among many companies. We will not lure your people, you will not take ours.

It is the escalator itself which increases the hang for loyalty. Each year, as it ascends, you earn a bit more and rise through the ranks with seniority. By the time you have been with the company ten years, you have a reasonable wage, an enhanced status and a fairly comfortable position. It would be unwise to risk that under any circumstances. But it would be particularly silly to do so by moving to another Japanese company. For then, you would probably have to start at or near the bottom and in a staff that does not like to absorb newcomers. That is quite different from the Western situation, where most change jobs in the expectation of yet more money, prestige and acceptance.

The lifetime employment system not only keeps most Japanese in their place, it enhances the desirability of entering large companies which can more readily provide lifetime employment. It adds to the attraction of growing companies, because they will find it easier to offer promotions and carry staff longer. Above all, it favors Japanese companies which are assumed to keep their employees come what may as opposed to Western or Asian companies which just hire and fire without regard to the employee's fate.

This presentation may not be as inspiring as the tale of the forty-seven *ronin* who followed their master even into death. But it does more to explain what foreign companies are likely to face when they seek Japanese personnel. For one, it will be much harder to recruit than in places where there is greater mobility. For another, most available candidates will be either rather young or rather old. And there may be some doubt about the future loyalty of any who happen to be available in mid-career.

While loyalty is real, but for different reasons than assumed, harmony (*wa*) seems to be more of a fiction. Certainly, there is harmony against everything outside the company. Within, however, it is quite another matter. Employees are jockeying for position so that they can take the escalator to the top and not be shoved off along the way. To do so, they frequently form factions whose struggle for power is as ruthless as anywhere in the world, though better concealed from public view. The stakes are high, namely the control of the only company they can work for.

You may assume this does not affect you. You are perhaps wrong. There may be one faction that likes working with your company and enjoys foreign exposure while another is more insular or just doesn't care for this particular relationship. Which faction comes out on top can be crucial for you as well, although I would not suggest mixing in company politics to affect the outcome. Still, if your guys lose, you had better start thinking of alternative arrangements.

It is obvious to anyone familiar with Japan that harmony is preached more fervently than it is practiced. Yet, you will hear ceaseless references to *wa*. They will come either from naive Westerners or devious Japanese.[2] The latter will suggest that you, the foreigner, should make every effort to get into line with Japanese mores, usually in a way that benefits them more than you. You may hear similar appeals for trust, human relations and so on. So, do pay lip-service, but don't let them take advantage of you. This is all part of the *tatemae* (illusion) and not the *honne* (reality) of Japanese being.

All is not well

This employment system, which defines the corporate culture in which most Japanese employees live, generates not only positive characteristics, like dedication, loyalty, hard work and so on. There are negative features as well. These failings are hardly ever referred to by the Japanese, since they either deny or hide them. Even most foreign observers have not noticed their existence. But they can be extremely important for foreign businessmen. Without wishing to overdo the parallel, it is the astute warrior who exploits his opponent's weaknesses. And it is necessary to seek them out.

One which may come as a surprise to most *gaijin*, who have never heard anything bad about Japanese workers, is that they are not as competent as might be desired. It is not just that I have personally met a large number of inefficient, sloppy or ignorant ones. They exist in abundance, just like everywhere else. What is more serious is that the system generates whole classes of incompetents.

You have doubtlessly heard of the Peter Principal according to which employees rise to the level of their incompetence. They are good at what they do, and get promoted to a position where they are also good, and then get promoted again. Somewhere along the line they get promoted too far and are incapable of handling the job. Now, this happens in an employment system where people are promoted on the basis (largely) of ability. Can you imagine what must happen when people are promoted on the basis (largely) of seniority?

The First Woronoff Principle is that Japanese are frequently unable to fulfill their responsibilities. They get promoted regularly, with the years, and a year older is not necessarily a year wiser. Worse, they get promoted into positions not on the basis of personal ability but the fact that the seat is empty because the former inhabitant was promoted further up. Not because they have been groomed for it, not because they have taken special training, not because they show a natural aptitude or anything else.

The Second Woronoff Principle, if this is not presumptuous, is that rotation generates large numbers of incompetents at all levels and all times. Clearly, when you are transferred to a new office, with new responsibilities and new colleagues, you cannot possibly know what to do. It takes time to learn. Most Japanese reckon about a year. They also feel that toward the third year, since you know you will soon be transferred out, employees tend to become slack and unconcerned. After all, come the next rotation and they will have left. That is pretty bad when you consider that employees may not be in their best form two years out of three.

On to the Third Woronoff Principle. Rotation has further drawbacks. I would be the first to admit that it forms employees with a profound knowledge of how the company operates. I already said that. But it is extremely difficult to develop professional knowhow when you are regularly shunted about, from personnel to sales, from sales to manufacturing, off to an overseas branch and back to a remote local subsidiary, and so on. And this in no logical order. It is thus impossible to develop any expertise or professionalism and even the Japanese concede this weakness.

Why then don't outsiders notice these weaknesses? To be perfectly frank, it is usually because foreigners are so starry-eyed and have been stuffed with such nonsense about Japanese efficiency by gullible academics that they cannot imagine that flaws exist, let alone look for them. But it can contribute greatly to your own effectiveness if you do realize that incompetence is alive and well in Japan, and not only the United States, France, the Philippines or wherever you come from.

For one, if things are actually being accomplished, then it may not be the person holding the formal title who is doing this but an assistant. There may be a junior employee who, either for love of the company, or affection for his superior, or because someone has to pitch in, actually assumes the responsibilities. He will earn Brownie points and perhaps rise to the top. That is a person you should cultivate.

Another pointer, when negotiating with the Japanese, do not assume that just because there is a pregnant silence the assembled businessmen are cogitating and coming up with a superlative response. They may just as well be puzzled and not know what to do. If you send a letter and don't get a reply, it may be because they cannot get their act together. If they do something stupid, it does not have to be a trap. It is not those wily Japanese who are trying to trick you. They can make mistakes, too. And you had better take advantage of them as they would benefit from your foolish moves.

On the other hand, don't complain about their blunders or tell them they are foolish. Protocol forbids. And the Japanese are particularly irked to be caught out or made to lose face. If you have the intelligence to realize that they goofed, have the tact not to say so outright.

Inefficiency amidst efficiency

Readers who have purchased Japanese cameras, or electronics, or automobiles may find it hard to believe that there is so much incompetence. The quality and price of these products seem to prove otherwise. But it must be remembered that the Japanese economy is very uneven, with a mixture of supremely efficient companies and others that would not make the grade anywhere else.

Efficiency is found mainly in larger companies, especially those in manufacturing. Inefficiency, alas, is encountered in many smaller companies and most other sectors, and in all companies among office workers as opposed to factory workers.

Blue-collar workers are well-trained. They are flexible, moving from job to job as necessary. Their machinery is productive and put to the best use. There is a constant effort to improve yet further, you know, *kaizen*.[3] Move the machinery a bit, change the design a bit, make your employees work a bit smarter, save a yen here and there and you are well ahead. If the work can be done better by machines, automate and bring in the robots. There will be no complaint from the workers who are either happy to get cleaner, safer jobs or are too dependent on the company to resist.

In addition, make the workers contribute to this effort. Obviously, nobody knows their job as well as they do and if anyone can suggest improvements, they can. So you form quality control circles and have them meet regularly to boost quality. You hold productivity campaigns and offer modest monetary rewards but ample prestige and promotions to get more suggestions. The workers cannot gripe if jobs are lost. After all, who made the suggestions?

You will not find much of this even in the administration of the same companies. White-collar workers are not organized as strictly, each man in his post, doing exactly what he should do, and con-stantly improving on that. They sit around in big, sprawling offices, with papers piled high on the desks and not even file cabinets to keep them in order. There are computers, but they are often off in a corner and operated by the lowly "office lady," since become a "computer lady." The more exalted male employees do not do that. In fact, they haven't discovered the telephone's usefulness yet. When they telephone, it is not to settle a business arrangement but to make an appointment.

White-collar employees spend an inordinate time with two activi-ties. One is to coordinate with colleagues. This involves such quaint practices as *ringi-sho* and *nemawashi*, dear to the hearts of foreign academics. The first is a written proposal by an underling which passes through the corporate hierarchy until everyone has signed on (i.e. put his personal seal on it). *Nemawashi* or "root-binding" involves endless one-on-one negotiations to obtain acceptance from everybody. And this means everybody. No such thing as a majority decision. Admirable ... if you are an academic. Horrible if you are trying to run a company efficiently.[4]

The other activity is to travel all over town, all over the country and all over the world to discuss business. The Japanese adore face-to-face encounters. They feel most comfortable working out details in person. They also like a chance to get out of the office and perhaps enjoy an interesting trip, hearty meals and cheerful drinking paid for by the company. Settle it by phone? Send a fax? Much too impersonal for the Japanese. But foreigners find it much cheaper, much faster, much more efficient. Another place where we are one up on the Japanese.

Not only are the offices inefficient, so are the distribution networks. As will be seen later, there are more wholesalers and retailers per customer in Japan than other advanced countries. Not only a bit more. About twice as many. This is sheer inefficiency. It adds tremendously to costs and involves more people in shifting products rather than making them. One reason Japan has succeeded is that it could sell many of its efficiently produced manufactures in efficient Western and Asian outlets, combining its strength with ours. Alas, we have to sell *our* goods through *their* distributors, which is not half as nice.

When it comes to inefficiency – as normally measured – there is nothing more inefficient than Japan's services. And the inefficiency increases the closer you get to the end user, especially the ordinary consumer. They demand "service," which sounds fair. Of course, they have a right to prompt delivery, perhaps also nice wrapping paper and pretty boxes, even after-sales service if the thing breaks down. But, and this is less sensible, they tend to favor establishments with superfluous and supercilious personnel. They want people to bow and scrape and treat them as exalted customers, which boosts their egos but not the nation's productivity.

So much for Japanese efficiency. Yes, efficiency in the factory. Efficiency in parts of banking. Efficiency in modern services. But not much to be seen in distribution or more traditional services. And, as I indicated in *Japan's Wasted Workers*, no managers enrolled in QC circles or making useful suggestions. That is for lesser mortals.

Again, how does this affect you, the foreigner? Well, if the Japanese are as good as claimed at manufacturing, you had better improve your own performance. On the other hand, if you are in distribution, the services or even parts of manufacturing they have neglected, you may well be more efficient than they are. You may know some tricks they do not. You may be able to outclass them.

Hierarchy above all

There is one last cultural feature which must never be forgotten. This undergirds and overarches all the others. It is hierarchy. This is a silent principle. It is not expressly stated and may actually be downplayed. Much of it has traditional roots, but a lot was concocted by management more recently. While it can be spontaneous, if one does not comply voluntarily compulsion can be used. Whatever the cause, the effect is that everybody in Japan knows his position in the hierarchy and this explains much of what he or she does.

Hierarchy takes many forms. Many, many forms. Perhaps more surprising in a company setting is the role of seniority. I said seniority, not age. What counts is how long a person has been with the company, not how old he is, and a recent transferee will have to bow to younger men who have been with the company longer. Another good reason not to engage in job hopping. Age only counts for things like retirement and birthdays (you are allowed to have those).

Seniority is not an abstract concept. It is worked into the employment system. As noted, employees rise gradually over the years. Later on, some attain high positions. The others tend to leave since it is hard to take orders from a junior. Senior and junior are not just sociological terms, each has to interact with the other in specified ways, using certain words, adopting expected attitudes, bowing in the prescribed manner. There is never any doubt who is the superior so, when managers walk about factories or sit in the common canteen, ordinary workers never have any doubt who they are.

Discrimination by sex also exists. Women, as noted, are much less likely to be promoted or even to stay with the company very long. But that is not all. They, too, are expected to behave, speak and bow appropriately, namely in a way that demeans them and exalts their male colleagues. In most cases, this implies even younger male colleagues although now some women have attained a position that outranks ordinary workers.

Race does not play much of a role since the Japanese are, or at least claim to be, homogeneous. Of course, the Japanese of Korean and Chinese origin are somewhat less homogeneous. The same applies for previous condition of servitude, except for the *burakumin* whose increasingly remote ancestors were in the wrong trades. Now, however, there is an added complication in that foreigners have to be integrated in the hierarchy. They include laborers from Asia and even further afield, skilled and unskilled, Westerners who simply decided to stay and mostly hold white-collar jobs, and executives posted here by foreign companies. This is a rather broad mix of *gaijin* and they will quickly learn that they are not all treated alike.

Beyond this hierarchy of persons there is a hierarchy of companies. Big companies certainly enjoy more prestige than smaller ones that do not work with them. Smaller ones that are subsidiaries, suppliers or subcontractors are in a distinctly inferior position. Suppliers in general, companies engaged in distribution, services and the like are always beholden to the exalted customer, be it an individual or corporate entity. This difference in status not only affects the company *per se* but any person who represents it, from top to bottom. Finally, those in business are on a lower rung than bureaucrats. It is hard to tell where politicians fit in ... but it is not very high up.

Nothing could be more mistaken than to assume that, as a foreign businessman, this may be culturally interesting but of no practical significance. Quite to the contrary. You are also expected to know your rank (or that of your company) and to abide by the proper etiquette. The Japanese will doubtlessly realize that you are not fully aware of the pecking order, cannot judge your exact position and may not know the fine points of formal conduct. They will expect some uncertainty and awkwardness. But transgressing the rules too blatantly would be courting disaster no matter what you are selling or how important your company is back home.

5
Choosing the Right Vehicle

There are two basic facts about the Japanese market that nobody seems to question. The Japanese market is one of the most attractive in the world. It is also one of the toughest in the world. Depending on whether the pull or push is greater, you should decide on how to approach doing business there. But you should certainly not be put off by its toughness and what you regard as your inability to crack it. There is more than one way of getting in and some of the ways are much less exacting than others.

The various entry points are discussed here, starting with the simpler ones like exporting, licensing and franchising. These are routes that are open to the smallest of companies with an interesting product or service and which wants to leave the hard part to Japanese agents. Next in line is joint venturing, which makes considerably greater demands on the foreign partner but still leaves major, usually more unfamiliar, functions to a Japanese partner. Going it alone by setting up a wholly owned operation is the most challenging, and sometimes most rewarding, alternative.[1]

Foreign companies should pick the vehicle which they think meets their needs and for which they have adequate resources. A joint venture or wholly owned subsidiary is more costly not only in time but also money. It may take some while, and considerable expense, to justify it. Just exporting, licensing or franchising can be arranged much faster and the returns materialize more quickly. However, the bigger rewards will still probably flow to those making the bigger effort.

So, it is also a question of commitment. Companies which are strongly committed to the Japanese market will choose the latter alternatives, even if they initially start with the former. But that does not mean that companies with less commitment must necessarily be excluded, as some supposed "experts" insist.

In the discussion of the various vehicles, the reader will soon notice that there are not only advantages but drawbacks to each. That is not quibbling. Nor is it a subtle warning. This is not a question of absolutes but tradeoffs. Once you have decided to go ahead, you must weigh the pros and cons to determine which is the best compromise. If you are looking for pat formulas or ideal solutions, you should try another book.

Just exporting

Exporting is a fairly standard, comparatively straightforward approach. It is not mentioned in most books on doing business in Japan, whose authors prefer more heroic endeavors. Still, it meets the basic requirement of selling your product in a market where there may be a demand and where success, even relative success, can be quite rewarding.

Of course, to enhance any chances of success, it is helpful to carefully choose the product. Some companies have only one. But others possess an array and one may do considerably better than the rest. This can be ascertained by market research, whether based on a reading of trade publications, visit to Japan, or full-blown study undertaken by a local consulting office. It would be wise to consider whether slight modifications in the product might not adapt it more to local conditions and thereby further increase sales potential.

Choosing the product is the first step. The second, frequently the most fateful one, is choosing the agent. For, once you have contracted a Japanese agent, most of the other steps will be taken by it, namely the choice of local distributors and outlets, pricing, positioning, advertising and so on. You may be able to offer advice, but don't count on it being followed to the letter. Moreover, since the agent knows the market so much better than you, don't be overly certain that you are right or it is wrong.

There are two basic options: general trading companies (*sogo shosha*) and specialized trading companies (*senmon shosha*). You should decide between them on the basis of the type of product, prospective sales, degree of technical know-how required, extent to which you want feedback, and so on.

The general trading companies or *sogo shosha* are best know abroad.[2] They get most of the publicity, both of their own making and articles by impressionable journalists and academics. After all, they are truly gigantic, with billions of dollars of annual turnover, thousands of employees, enormous financial resources and offices spanning the globe. While there is some specialization, they are amazingly diversified, carrying literally thousands of different products from Japan to dozens of foreign countries and the other way around.

While most of the literature stresses their export prowess, they also import huge amounts of goods into Japan. In fact, imports account for more of their turnover than do exports and they control about a fifth of total wholesaling volume. In Japan, they have associates and subsidiaries which process many raw materials, manufacture assorted articles, or engage in distribution of goods. On the whole, they emphasize bulk products, including raw materials and other commodities, but they also handle large capital goods and larger consumer items as well as some services.

That means a *sogo shosha* may be suitable for your purposes. However, before even approaching one, remember that these large and variegated entities may not provide customized service which meets your needs. In addition, they will not even bother with your products unless a (rather large) minimum turnover can be expected. And, on the whole, they are somewhat less specialized than their smaller counterparts.

If a general trading company seems appropriate, you can usually start looking for one without even leaving home. You can contact the local JETRO office, which has directories providing information about the nine *sogo shosha* and their activities and will help you decide which is strongest in your line of business. You could then perhaps visit the trader's local office, since they have so many. If there is none conveniently located, you could write to the head office in Tokyo for an initial approach. If the prospects are interesting, someone will be sent to visit you. If not, as they say, "don't call us, we'll call you."

If your product is rather complicated, if you need more customized service, if you can only sell a limited amount or your company is fairly small, you are probably better off with a special-ized trading company or *senmon shosha*. It will be able to meet your needs better and, being a small company itself, is unlikely to lord it over you. But it will still want to know that your product is promis-ing, that there is a potential market, and that it can distribute the article properly. These are exactly the same questions you should be asking yourself. For, this time, with 10,000 *senmon shosha*, there is an enormous field to choose from and you have to get it right.

These smaller traders vary tremendously amongst themselves in exact specialization, size and financial strength, access to distribu-tors and end-users and also ability to work with foreigners. Moreover, some are just traders and pass goods on to wholesalers while others are actually wholesalers with an international dimen-sion. In the list are several foreign firms, which may for that reason be more adapted to handling foreign products. They include Dodwell, Jardine, and Gadelius.

Finding the right importer will take some effort, but it is time and money well spent. First, you might make a call to the nearest JETRO office or send a letter to your embassy or chamber of commerce in Tokyo to make recommendations. It will not be easy to choose without actually going there and meeting with the representatives of several traders. While in Japan, you should look more carefully into how similar products are handled and perhaps chat with foreign counterparts who know them to find out which traders they are using and what the results have been. Do not hurry the process. Take as much time as you need to find the right agent the first time.

So far I have referred to quite commonplace aspects of doing busi-ness, things you must be familiar with from experiences in other countries. However, as noted in the previous chapter, Japan is dis-tinguished by particularly close relations between companies. So it is essential not only to determine whether a trader can do the job but whether it *will do the job*. That is, whether it may not make only half-hearted efforts due to a conflict of interests.

General trading companies are not only traders, they have sub-sidiaries which are manufacturers. If you produce the same thing as a subsidiary, they may not wish to deal with you at all or will give you second-rate treatment.[3] Some specialized traders are also manu-facturers or, if not, they are very closely related to manufacturers. They may also prove unsuitable. This means it is indispensable to do some serious research into the web of relations to discover whether such conflicts exist and, if so, give your preference to agents which are not bound this way.

Licensing and franchising

The Japanese market is very large. It is also very distant from most other countries. This means that it can be rather costly and also time-consuming to ship goods to Japan by sea or air. It may, under certain circumstances, be much cheaper to have them produced locally. That idea, by the way, is just as likely to occur to a Japanese company as the foreign one and, after considering the alternatives, they may decide that licensing is the best way to go.

The ideal partner for licensing, unlike exporting, is a manufacturer. But this time it is necessary to be even more selective. First, you have to check that the manufacturer can make the product competently and cheaply enough to sell locally. Then you have to determine whether it has access to suitable distribution channels. Finally, it is wise to find out if the product competes directly with one of its own or fills a gap. Your product does not have to be "unique," but it must round out the licensee's line if it is to receive strong support.

The situation for franchising is similar, except that it usually applies to services which could not be "exported" to Japan even if you wanted. You have to reproduce locally the same sort of establishment you have developed in your own country, one which is hopefully distinctive enough to attract Japanese customers. Since "foreignness" may actually be a key selling point, the possibilities are amazingly broad. In fact, franchising has been one of the most traveled and successful routes of late with entrants increasing from several dozen to several hundred. They include all the big names and some small, from McDonald's, Kentucky Fried Chicken and Seven-Eleven to France Croissant.

Still, to succeed here it is indispensable to find the right partner. This can be even more difficult than for manufacturing because it is not so easy to just hand over the plans and go ahead. You must be certain that the level of compliance with your instructions is adequate, not just once in a while through spot checks of franchises, but regularly from year to year, from location to location. On the other hand, you may have to adjust your own procedures even more to suit local tastes without, however, losing the crucial elements that make your operation distinctive.

The possible range of partners is somewhat wider. You can choose a counterpart, a department store for boutiques, another retailer for special convenience stores, a food processor or distributor for fast-food outlets, and so on. You can then count on a certain degree of familiarity with the sector, enough basic expertise to get started, and access to personnel, etc. Given the high cost of land, the best partner may be a company with large land holdings. Or, due to their many ramifications, a *sogo shosha* may prove suitable.[4]

As for exporting, you want an associate who cannot only do the job but will work hard at it. That is never easy to determine in advance. But a routine check on experiences of similar foreign firms and the relations with other Japanese companies is certainly in order.

Once again, a call to your local JETRO office, a look at the various directories, an examination of some of the trade publications, a letter to the embassy or foreign chamber may give you a pretty good idea of potential partners. Attending trade shows at home, or preferably in Japan, may establish contacts. But this is a sufficiently serious matter that you may want a consulting office to undertake studies. And you should personally visit, or send an appropriate mission to, Japan to meet with potential partners and negotiate a clear agreement with whichever appears best.

Among the other looser arrangements one might include what is glibly called "strategic alliances." They can involve almost anything from joint distribution, to joint production to joint research and development. What is truly interesting here is that the emphasis is switching from foreigners as the leaders to Japanese as equals or leaders. More and more, Japanese companies are coming up with products that foreigners would like to license. They are also engaging in advanced research, the results of which foreign companies would like to acquire. In some cases, they may find it best to get in at the ground floor through co-development.[5]

Joint venturing

Exporting, licensing and franchising are acceptable alternatives in their own terms. You export your products to Japan, as you do for Canada or France, and you get paid. You have your products manufactured in Japan and, in return for the specifications, instructions and rights, you get a royalty. You entrust your system to a Japanese franchisee and you receive mutually agreed fees. All this is very simple and straightforward. No hassle. No fuss. No need to figure out a complicated distribution network, bother with finicky clients or haggle with government officials. You don't even have to learn how to bow or use chopsticks.

But this is still a fairly low level of commitment. The returns are certainly attractive, but only commensurate with the input. Perhaps, if you did a bit more, the returns would be larger. Also, by upgrading your effort, you would certainly have more control over the operation. You would know who your customers are, what their requirements are, whether they are satisfied with your product or service. You would have more feedback. Also, from this level, it is rather hard to expand aside from entrusting more products or services to your agent or associate.

To increase control, enhance feedback, provide a basis for further growth, many foreign companies prefer taking an additional step. But they do not want to go it alone in a strange country they do not quite fathom. They prefer the alternative of a joint venture. Until the 1980s, they did not have much choice since investment was restricted. Now, despite the fact that 100% ownership is permitted, many still prefer this halfway house.[6]

This is justified by the "tough market" part of our equation. Some of the things that are particularly difficult about Japan include recruiting personnel, managing along Japanese lines and just buying or renting premises, given the exorbitant prices. But nothing seems harder than penetrating the distribution system. Finding the right channels, and then convincing the distributors to carry your products, can be such a daunting task that it puts off many otherwise eager businessmen.

Through a joint venture, the foreign company can share any efforts with a Japanese partner. The foreign side contributes the product, usually a rather special one (if not quite unique) in terms of price, quality or performance. It grants the rights and passes on the technologies. It also shares the financial burden. The Japanese side usually provides the rest of the finance, access to distribution channels, and perhaps manufacturing facilities. It may also "loan" the initial staff, supply premises and deal with the government.

Choosing the partner for a joint venture is a much more delicate matter than picking an importer or licensee. It is necessary to find another company that can get the job done, and do it in a way you thoroughly approve of since closer cooperation is inevitable. Since you will be sharing an office, sometimes also a factory, and staff, the degree of compatibility must be much greater. Also, your partner should make its very best efforts to sell the goods produced. So you cannot afford a conflict of interest, i.e. having a partner with close relations to one of your competitors or which itself produces something too similar.

Moreover, in the Japanese context, a joint venture is a very serious relationship, more comparable perhaps to an old-fashioned marriage where both sides must stick together through good and hard times. That derives from customs and traditions. It is enforced by the need to "save face," something that acutely concerns any Japanese company but should also interest you if your intention is to show deeper commitment and seek long-term benefits.

For many years, a joint venture was not only the best way to participate actively, it was the only way due to restrictions on investment. Yet, even now, many foreigners like it. If you establish one, you will be in good company along with leading joint ventures like Fuji Xerox, Nihon Unisys, Sumitomo 3M, Yamatake-Honeywell, McDonald's Japan, Toppan Moore, DuPont Toray, etc., etc. But this vehicle is losing some of its luster.

In fact, there is presently a lively debate about the future of joint ventures. They are no longer imposed and some of what they offered can be obtained in other ways. More to the point, many were mediocre successes and some were outright failures. The explanation may be that, as was noted by Jackson N. Huddleston, Jr., a perceptive businessman and consultant, "many joint ventures have been shotgun weddings; neither side got what it wanted. The Japanese wanted a licensing agreement and the foreigner, especially Americans, wanted a wholly owned subsidiary."[7] Still, as he conceded, joint ventures continue to be formed to reduce costs or access distribution. Even today, the joint venture remains the principal form of cooperation.

This means that foreign companies should not only consider the possible advantages but any conceivable drawbacks and make every effort to avoid them. Much has been written on what goes into making a successful joint venture. Some of the better advice has come from Mark Zimmerman, who ran several during his years in Japan. Here are some of the factors he regarded as crucial:

> First, there must be a definite product, technology, marketing system, or brand that the partnership can immediately and profitably develop and exploit. Second, the Western firm must have a clear understanding with the Japanese partner regarding short-, medium- and long-range objectives and profit expectations. Third, the foreign partner has to be prepared for a relatively long payout period, and to accommodate this fact in its calculations when establishing financial objectives. Fourth the foreign partner must remember that the Japanese look upon a joint venture as more than a simple business arrangement. They will view it just as they do their relationships with suppliers, distributors, agents or trading companies – as a relationship of trust that is expected to endure the test of time.[8]

Going it alone

Many foreign companies are worried about possible conflicts of interest and do not really trust Japanese counterparts. They may also hold proprietary rights to truly exceptional technologies they do not want to part with, not even to a carefully chosen partner. In some instances, the management philosophy emphasizes going it alone in all markets, domestic and overseas, and growing a venture from a small beginning rather than starting with a full-fledged one.

In such cases, a wholly owned subsidiary is certainly preferred. What is more, it is increasingly easy to arrange in Japan aside from a very few sectors. This, however, means that the foreign company is saddled with certain problems a joint venture can avoid or at least simplify. They include the need to establish your own office, recruit your own personnel, handle your own distribution – subjects that will be dealt with in greater detail elsewhere. The financial demands are also greater. In return, any rewards should be that much larger because they do not have to be shared with a partner. That is another reason why the wholly owned venture beckons.

Yet, even if you take this route, it is possible to advance step by step. The very first step could be to set up a representative office.

This could be a rather small, if fairly well-appointed (and expensive) office, with only one or two expatriates and some secretaries. It might do little more than follow events in the sector to know what your competitors are doing and give advance warning of new products or strategies.

Such an operation would be yet more useful if it kept an eye on your importers and distributors, to see how good a job they are doing and increase the feedback. This should obviously not just be filed. It should be used to encourage greater efforts on their part, since they know you are watching. It could also be used advantageously to adapt your products to customer wishes.

This office could also seek additional products which might then be exported to or produced in Japan. Most larger companies have a whole array and the first one they tried may not even have been the best. With a local operation, it is much easier to undertake appropriate market research to find the right product. It could also get a much better feel for the appropriate distributors and probably negotiate better conditions.

The next phase might be a branch office or actual subsidiary. Its initial focus could be improving distribution. This might involve adding new distributors to the old (or more rarely replacing them) so as to cover a broader territory. You could perhaps provide greater backup in terms of point-of-sale material or advertising. It would already be a much bigger step if you were to create your own distribution network, but one certain companies eventually find necessary. Other major strides would be to go over to local manufacturing and conceivably research and development.

All of these things are much, much, much easier said than done. And there will be times when you wish you had a partner. But, if you really want to become an active player and more of an insider, you must make the effort. This is a high-stakes game, but the route requiring the biggest commitment also offers the greatest potential.

How you set up a corporation is something much better discussed with a lawyer or judicial scrivener (*shiho shoshi*). But it should be mentioned in passing that the more formal "stock company" known as *kabushiki kaisha* or K.K. is not the only alternative. It is also possible to establish a limited liability company known as *yugen-kaisha* or Y.K. Helene Thian suggested the latter for small businesses, since it is easier to adopt and requires fewer formalities. She also opts for the scrivener as cheaper than a lawyer.[9]

While not yet a majority, wholly owned operations are increasingly popular and accessible. This category boasts many of the big names like IBM, Coca-Cola, Esso, Nestlé, Digital Equipment, Intel, Hoechst and BMW. But there are also legions of tiny ventures, often launched by a single foreigner, who is out there on his own. Like the one I ran, they have to make up for size with speed and they cannot afford to wait for the Japanese side to come to a decision on every detail.

For foreign companies in a rush, and without the time to grow a Japanese operation, or those which want to start big, there is finally another alternative. That is to acquire a Japanese company, something almost impossible only a decade ago, and now fairly common. This option is discussed more fully in the next chapter.

Consultants

This is a good point to return to an intermediary that was already mentioned in passing several times, the consultant. A consulting office in Japan can accomplish many useful tasks for the newcomer and even companies which are long established. The right one can smooth over so many difficulties and open so many doors that it can spell the difference between success and failure. If you get stuck with the wrong one, you would be much better off alone.

As already noted, a consulting office can do some essential basic research. It can, first of all, undertake market research itself or through a more specialized company in order to know more exactly the prospects for your product, how it should be marketed, what distributors should be used, and so on. It can check on your competitors to see whether they have similar products and how theirs compare. Even more important, it can participate actively in the search for suitable importers, licensees, franchisees or joint venture partners.

To establish the formal relations, a consultant can be particularly useful. It could fulfil the function of go-between in a society where even couples who have known one another for years want a go-between to officiate at their marriage. It is much easier for a consultant not only to seek a partner but to introduce you to such a partner, acting on your behalf but still more or less as a third party. It can then advise you on how to negotiate a deal, what conditions might prove acceptable, how to behave and so on. If the negotiations drag on, and you have to return home, it is important to have someone around who can follow up. While good news will be readily forthcoming, it may be easier for the consultant to coax out any bad news.

If you opt for exporting, licensing or franchising, you may not feel it is worthwhile establishing even a small permanent office. A consultant's office can probably do some of the follow-up, either by assigning a dedicated staff member or working on a case-by-case basis. Should you go further and set up an office, you may wish to locate it in a corner of the consultant's suite or have an outside one operated by the consultant. If you go ahead with a larger project, be it a joint venture or wholly owned subsidiary, the consultant can at least provide advice on where to find premises, what the going rates are, etc. If you want to recruit personnel, it could help find them or suggest a head-hunter to aid you.

Since the consultant can be so important, it is essential to pick the right one. That is not easy. But it is certainly much easier than selecting Japanese partners. For most of the consultants are foreigners, or used to working with foreigners, whether specialists or retired businessmen. You will at least find no great culture gap. You can also more readily get information on their previous experiences by checking with the embassy, foreign chamber or other foreign businessmen.

Conditions are fairly standard and rates can be negotiated. This may evolve into a long relationship but it can also be restricted to certain periods or services.

Still, it should not be forgotten that consultants – even when under contract with and paid by you – can have personal interests that do not entirely coincide with yours.

For one, they tend to prefer companies which keep a lower profile and do not set up a local office because then they are much more dependent on the consultant for information, advice and other paid services. If you wish to upgrade your operation, they may well suggest a joint venture rather than a wholly owned operation because you would again be in greater need of backup for a longer time. Probably the last thing they would do is tell you to give up on Japan. No, they will suggest alternative products, partners, approaches to keep you around and in their clientele.

That is all comprehensible. Consultants do the same thing everywhere. In Japan, there is a further wrinkle. Some consultants have greater affinity to certain Japanese companies or groups than others. Given the difficulty in establishing relations, they might steer you toward those they are familiar with. Alas, they may not be the right ones. So, it is best you check whether the consultant tends to favor the same source for tie-ups and, more important, whether this is indeed a suitable partner for you. That must be through your own sleuthing or the work of another consultant.

Pointers on partnering

In connection with all of the various alternatives, there are certain strategic factors which should never be forgotten. They were occasionally hinted at but certainly deserve more specific treatment and, if necessary, repetition. All of them tie up with the concept of "partnering", which I hear endlessly. Foreign businessmen are busily seeking partners to import, distribute, license, franchise, manufacture, cooperate on research, etc. The ultimate form of partnership is apparently the joint venture.

Personally, I do not like the expression. I think it is not only misplaced, it can actually be misleading and get you in trouble if you assume the Japanese understand it in the same way as *gaijin*. Actually, the Japanese have no special liking or predisposition for such an arrangement. Partners are related in an often rather loose manner; the Japanese prefer stricter, more structured, relationships. Partners can be changed from time to time; the Japanese seek long-term associations. Above all, partners are roughly equal, no matter how big or important one may be compared to another. This clashes with the Japanese hang for hierarchy.

Another problem is that "partnering" has a warm, mushy, emotional quality, what the Japanese call "wet." This is supposed to involve more than just doing business together. There is an element of common challenge plus a note of possible friendship. No matter how much the Japanese fancy "wet" relationships and love to drink, chat and sing *karaoke* songs even with *gaijin* guests, it would be unwise to assume that they are partners, let alone friends. The relationship is strictly business and letting emotional overtones arise only deludes and weakens the foreign side.

Yet, foreign businessmen are constantly creating partnerships, many of which they are later surprised to find were not only flimsy but worked against them. Their Japanese partners, despite all the talk of "trust" and "human relations," failed to provide the inputs expected, reneged on agreements about prices or profits, and dilly-dallied on virtually everything. Worse, in some cases they copied the product and dumped the provider. That is certainly not how a partner should act!

Well, if they did not want this to happen, the *gaishi* should have thought about it earlier and taken appropriate precautions. Some, actually rather few, can be written into the contract. The others must be enforced by keeping an eye on the partnership and reminding the Japanese side of what is expected. This means not leaving too many decisions to your partner and looking for alternatives if things should sour. But much of this could be obviated if foreign companies reflected seriously on a few crucial points when picking partners.

For one, should you choose a partner who is in the same business or not? Obviously, for reasons of effectiveness, the former is more attractive. You will cooperate with another company which has experience in your sector, has distributors used to working there, knows how to produce your line of goods, and so on. Alas, this means it could conceivably clone your product and get along without you one of these days. Cooperation with a distributor, manufacturer or other company in another sector, while more complicated, may be safer.

So far, the vast majority of tie-ups were between likes: automaker with automaker, pharmaceutical firm with pharmaceutical firm, food processor with food processor, and so on. But one of the most significant success stories is Schick, which has its razor blades distributed through a company in the watch business. Other examples are Allstate Life Insurance whose policies are sold in Seibu's stores, and Pier 1 Imports whose home furnishing stores are run with a partner in the printing business, Akatsuki.

The second strategic choice is whether to work with a large, prestigious company or a smaller one. Again, the first is more appealing. It has a grander reputation, greater resources, broader distribution network, firmer government contacts, etc. Yet, this is the kind of partner which not only could dominate you, in a hierarchical society it may almost inevitably do so. Perhaps you would be better off with a company more your size or even smaller, one you could conceivably dominate.

The third question is whether to cooperate with a group or *keiretsu* as an "honorary" member of sorts by tying up with one of its participants. There are definite advantages, and they should not be underestimated. This would almost automatically open up sales possibilities. If would also make it easier to come by financing, obtain reliable suppliers and so on. The flip side is that, once within one group, it would be impossible to penetrate others. It might thus be best to remain outside although initially it will be harder to get by.

The fourth alternative, and this option is still fairly new and limited in scope, is whether to tie up with a purely Japanese partner or take one which is partly foreign. In practice, this usually means tying up with a *gaishi* that is itself part of a joint venture or sometimes wholly-owned. Thus, Toys Я Us in Japan is partly owned by McDonald's Japan, and Hill's (for pet food) is a wholly-owned affiliate of Colgate-Palmolive (Japan). The advantage is that your partner (or owner) is basically on the same wavelength and cooperation should be more smoother. The drawback is that your partner is itself, in many cases, not fully integrated in the Japanese economy and/or to some extent dependent on its own Japanese partner.

These are four essential strategic decisions which must be made when picking a "partner." All too often, they are overlooked by newcomers who stumble into arrangements which will influence their whole future and are extremely hard to reverse. I will not prejudge the answers. They should depend on the requirements of the foreign side and, as noted, there are pluses and minuses both ways. But at least do not forget about them in the hustle and bustle of getting into Japan.

At any rate, since relations with Japanese "partners" are of such consequence, it is essential to make them as positive as possible. It is therefore worthwhile considering the views of one businessman who has thought long and hard about the subject. That is T.W. Kang whose "guidelines for a successful partnership" follow:

> Balance global and local motives for partnering. Pick a compatible partner. Negotiate hard for return, but only in the context of

a positive relationship for both parties; and structure the relationship properly. Commit the necessary resources to the execution of the partnership. Accept differences in culture. Develop credibility on both sides. Follow established principles of management. Keep contacts at high levels. Anticipate problems. Be flexible and willing to adjust.[10]

6
Mergers and Acquisitions

About a decade ago, when the first edition of this book was written, the alternative of actually buying up or buying into a Japanese company hardly existed. Indeed, mergers and acquisitions (M&A) were regarded as almost a dirty trick, the sort of thing devious foreigners might do with one another, but hardly something that Japanese should engage in amongst themselves. And the idea of a foreign company taking over a Japanese one was considered even more heinous, like a second coming of the "black ships." Even foreigners thought such a thing was a bit improbable.

This was not due only to a dislike of the practice. There were many cultural barriers. The strongest was that, in Japanese business folklore and somewhat also in practice, a company supposedly belonged to its employees and could thus not be bought and sold like an object. Of course, the employees could agree to such a transaction. But they were very unlikely to agree to it when the acquirer was foreign. This doubtlessly had something to do with a broader, more diffuse dislike and distrust of foreign businessmen. Any such feelings, however, were strongly reinforced by seeing what foreigners did when they acquired companies, including various forms of restructuring and downsizing which involved changing the shape of the company as known by its present employees and then sacking some of them. Hardly the sort of practice that appealed to personnel promised lifetime employment.

There were other obstacles to takeovers as well. One was an entrenched management which, aside from fear of being sacked, saw no particular interest in selling even if this meant the new company would be more efficient and profitable. For profit was not rated very highly as a goal. As long as they could muddle through, and earn enough to cover costs, they preferred leaving well enough alone. Then there were the many other shareholders, including banks and members of the broader *keiretsu*, which could resist a takeover. Under Japanese law, minority shareholders are not obliged to sell even if the majority agrees to a deal, although this may change. There would also obviously be pressure from suppliers and distributors, namely the links up and down within company *keiretsu*, which could at least exert (moral) pressure. Last but not least, the bureaucrats, especially those of the Ministry of Finance, could use various devices to prevent takeovers if they wished, which they usually did. This made a friendly takeover difficult and a hostile one nearly impossible.

Still, over the 1990s, the situation changed, and will continue changing as Japan's economy slowly and grudgingly moves into line with the other advanced economies. The biggest nudge has actually come from the recession. Once upon a time, Japanese companies were so financially solid and technologically advanced that they did not think they needed anything from foreign companies. But many of Japan's major firms have fallen on hard times and countless lesser ones are fairly desperate. They were terribly short of money which might be obtained through a tie-up. Worse, they could not invest in as much R&D, and are thus also short of new products. Meanwhile, foreign companies often have excess cash which they would gladly invest to gain or expand a presence in Japan.

Naturally, this imbalance will decrease as Japan's economy recovers and other economies slow down. But there is another factor, often overlooked, which should remain intact much longer. While Japan has many large companies, which might be hard to take over, it also has masses of smaller ones which are really quite tiny compared to foreign rivals and could be acquired. Even the large companies are not as large as they used to be. In absolute terms, Japanese banks, brokerages, insurers, manufacturers and others have been shrinking over the past decade. Meanwhile, foreign counterparts have been growing. This is partly due to the M&A boom abroad which created giants that now tower over even Japan's top firms.

The increased openness to M&A, the relative financial strength and the size of foreign firms, and the willingness of the bureaucracy to permit such transactions, have resulted in an M&A boomlet in Japan, nothing much compared to the United States, but substantial in Japanese terms. In 1998 there were about a hundred cases of foreign companies buying Japanese ones, about half as many as the cases of Japanese buying foreign companies and a fifth that of Japanese buying Japanese, but almost ten times as much in all cases as in 1990.[1] From an insignificant level at the start of the decade, foreign acquisitions were exceeding a total of two trillion yen at the end.[2] Moreover, while most of the earlier deals were fairly small, they grew over the years until even a $1 billion deal was not uncommon.

These deals covered a growing range of sectors. The earliest, already back in the 1980s, often involved pharmaceutical companies. A notable example was Merck's takeover of Banyu. Another earlier and ongoing effort was Ford's gradual absorption of Mazda and General Motors' stake in Isuzu. More recently Bosch acquired a controlling interest in Zexel, an automobile parts maker. Great Britain's Bass bought a hotel chain from Saison Group. AT&T and British Telecommunications together took a share in Japan Telecom and Britain's Cable & Wireless first seized a controlling stake (53%) in International Digital Communications through a rare hostile takeover and than raised it to nearly 98%. Merrill Lynch bought some assets of Yamaichi Securities, the failed Japanese broker, and Traveler's Group of a healthier Nikko. The biggest deal, and one that would not have been believed before it happened, was Renault's purchase of 36.8% of Nissan, Japan's second largest automaker, for $5.4 billion.

Where an outright acquisition was not possible, either because the Japanese partner was still strong or did not like to admit weakness, various other forms of "alliances" could be conceived. In one, Toshiba entered into an agreement with Electrolux to increase the latter's access to the Japanese market in a limited number of areas. In the arrangement between Sumitomo Tire and Goodyear, the world market was divided into six regions, in five of which Goodyear had a majority stake, while Sumitomo remained the senior partner in Japan. Meanwhile Volvo and Mitsubishi Motors joined forces for truck production and sales. Countless other alliances involved Japanese companies manufacturing and/or marketing goods for foreign companies so as to make fuller use of existing capacity.

What is on offer?

Now that acquiring a Japanese company is a real possibility, many foreign companies will find this is a preferable option to the ones mentioned before, whether exporting or franchising, or working out an arrangement with a Japanese company, which can involve a joint venture but one with a very different flavor from the joint ventures arising out of M&A. After all, just by paying over a sum of money, assets which would have had to be accumulated painstakingly over the years or even decades can be obtained right off. And the Japanese partner, or so it might seem, would be grateful for the chance and certainly less picky than in the past.

But exactly what can be obtained? Obviously, the more successful companies are not on offer. This includes most of those with relatively solid management, reasonably sound finances, first-rate technologies and well-known brand names. But ever since the acquisition of Nissan, even top firms are within the realm of possibility, although only when they have substantial debts. In short, it is mainly companies which are in serious difficulty that are open to offers. But there are lots of these. During the "bubble economy" of the 1980s, there was no end to the companies which expanded excessively, and sometimes recklessly, going into all sorts of activities far from their core and in which they did poorly. There was also excessive investment in overseas operations and property at home and abroad. These companies ran up huge debts, in the hundreds of trillions of yen for the lot, and they are a crushing burden. Indeed, the average debt equity ratio is 4:1, very high and very debilitating.

That is what happened in the manufacturing sector and also in services, with banks, brokerages and insurance companies opening too many branches and taking on too much staff. They also financed many of the activities above of their clients, which when they collapsed dragged down their financiers, which were stuck with unrecoverable loans and all sorts of assets, from property to paintings, they could not possibly sell for a decent price. Thus, many players in the financial sector are also open to offers. In fact, even the Ministry of Finance is out soliciting for them.

While many of the larger, older, more prestigious companies are strapped for cash, they can usually get by by squeezing their suppliers, distributors and other associates. There is also a tendency to expect government support, although this is not always forthcoming. So they are not quite desperate, in most cases. Smaller companies certainly are. They have no one to fall back on, whether associates or the government, or the banks for that matter, and they must pay their debts or go under. There is an enormous number of these. In fact, while Japan is regarded as a country of big companies by those not overly familiar with it, 99% of the total are small and medium enterprises. They include, according to the Ministry of International Trade and Industry, 11 car companies, 79 tire companies, 72 oil companies, 1,069 pharmaceutical companies, 2,083 gas companies and 5,808 steel companies. There are also masses of small fry in the services.

Yet, while many of the above probably are desperate, and would not turn down a proper offer, they cannot simply be stalked and taken over as in the West. Hostile takeovers are still very hard to engineer. This is partly because the business culture strongly disapproves of them, partly because the legislation creates impediments. The principal one is that minority shareholders cannot be forced to sell even when a majority is in favor. And it is often possible to mobilize a blocking minority among shareholders in the company itself, including the founder and staff, or among other companies related through *keiretsu* or other traditional business ties.

Even if the takeover is friendly, it may not be possible to acquire 100% of the stock. There will probably always be shareholders which do not want to sell out, perhaps for sentimental reasons, or to maintain some influence in the new entity, or simply because they want a higher (and unacceptable) price. The legislation does not oblige them to sell, at least at present, although that may change, and there is no way of forcing them out.

More to the point, it may not even be advantageous to have 100% ownership. There are benefits to having the founder and staff, suppliers and distributors, and other firms in a broader group, maintain a vested interest in the company's success even under new and foreign management. Less palpably, there can be advantages to preserving a Japanese element in the company so that, to the public and the personnel, it retains a Japanese cachet. Japanese customers still tend to favor local to foreign products in most cases; a partially local company blends in better with the trade associations and may enjoy better treatment by the bureaucracy. Likewise, Japanese employees still prefer working for an at least partially Japanese company. Indeed, in some undefinable way, a company could lose its "soul" and, although this is not normally counted in the assets, it should be.

There are various alternatives to 100% ownership. It is possible to have a controlling interest with just over 50% or, in practice, even somewhat less depending on the shareholder structure. An alternative is a 33.4% holding which makes it possible to veto any decision of the board of directors. This is enough, if not to determine all policy, at least to avoid any undesirable decisions. And it has the advantage of not consolidating the acquired company's losses and liabilities. This solution was adopted by Renault. Other lesser levels provide smaller degrees of control, and are perfectly valid if the goal is more cooperation than control.

Thus, the situation is somewhat ambivalent. For the first time in postwar Japanese history, foreign companies can fairly readily acquire Japanese companies. This includes companies of all sorts, in all sectors, and even some very fine ones which have come upon hard times. On the other hand, these companies are often loaded with debt. They have also obviously made some rather serious mistakes on essential policies. So, should any possibilities be followed up? That will obviously depend on each individual case, with the main determinants being the cost, the benefits and the risks.

What does it cost?

There is no doubt about it, by the end of the 1990s most Japanese companies looked cheaper than they had been in a very, very long time. The shares of those on the stock market had fallen by about half, some less, others considerably more. Private companies would have lost about as much value, if not more, since they were usually financially weaker. In addition, the yen itself had slipped against the dollar, most European currencies and the euro. Companies could thus be acquired for as little as a quarter to a third as much as before.

This was a definite buying opportunity. And there was no knowing how long it would last. After all, Japan's stock market would not remain depressed forever. Similarly, the yen was bound to gather strength as Japan again sought to export itself out of a recession. Thus, the costs were bound to rise although part of this rise would be justified by an improved operating and financial situation. So there might be bargains around for a while.

Still, what is a bargain? Should you buy the cheapest companies? Probably not. They were also the most distressed ones, closest to bankruptcy, and with problems no acquirer could solve fast enough. It is doubtlessly wiser to pay a bit more for a company in better shape. Alas, from outside, it is extremely difficult to know just how valuable a Japanese company is.

The handiest guide is the stock market, for those companies whose shares are traded. This is certainly a very imperfect guide, since many companies are closely held by *keiretsu* associates which do not sell, and the market has been manipulated on occasion. At least, it is possible to get a very rough valuation. It is also easier to determine which companies have fallen most, avoiding them, and sticking to those which fared somewhat better.[3]

Why bother with such a rough estimate when there are banks and credit-rating agencies which are there to provide more precise figures? Unfortunately, in this respect, Japan remains Japan. It is extremely hard for any outsider to know just what is going in a Japanese company, and if the bank or credit-rating agency is outside the *keiretsu*, it probably won't really know the situation. On the other hand, if it is an associate, it will probably not tell and would tend to accentuate the positive while overlooking the negative. By the way, auditors' reports are not much use either. Japanese auditors usually accept whatever information they are given without checking too closely. You are thus faced with the views of those who don't know or of those who do know but won't say.

What about the company's accounts and statements? They are not terribly helpful since the accounting rules are terribly lax to begin with, and the accountants are extremely astute when it comes to putting a positive spin on the situation. Often debt is shuffled up and back among affiliates in order to make the parent company look good while assets are reported at artificially high rates and liabilities at low ones. It is easy enough to realize things are worse, but how much worse is hard to tell as liabilities are carefully hidden. Admittedly, there has been some improvement over the years. Japanese firms, especially those whose stock is traded abroad, do provide more revealing accounts. They have begun to include various subsidiaries in consolidated accounts. And the government itself is pressing for more transparency. But for the moment most accounts are not worth the paper they are written on.

If you want to know just what the financial situation is, you have to find out for yourself. So send in the accountants from the head office, but be certain they are accompanied by local accountants who know Japanese practices and tricks. Have them go through the accounts of the target company, and also of any subsidiary or affiliate for which it may be accountable. They should consider not only any debts or liabilities for which the company is legally responsible, but even those for which it has a moral obligation due to some promise or time-honored practice. They should also look into any obligations toward the personnel, including the pension fund which is most often inadequately funded.

The reason for being particularly careful is that the cost will consist of two parts: what is actually paid for the company today and what must be paid tomorrow to sop up any hidden debts and liabilities.

There is a third element to cost which should be borne in mind. In America and even Europe many mergers are financed by swapping shares. This is not usually done in Japan. In addition, when it does occur, it is heavily taxed. So the purchase is more likely to be entirely or largely in cash. But it will not be easy, perhaps not even possible, to find a Japanese bank to underwrite the operation, although foreign banks may be more amenable. These far from petty financing expenses must be included in any calculation.[4]

What is it worth?

What a company costs is not quite the same thing as what it is worth. Moreover, while the price may be more or less the same for all potential acquirers – assuming they are equally astute negotiators – it will be worth considerably more or less to each one of them. This depends on what they can get out of the arrangement. The difference usually hinges on whether they obtain two of the most essential keys to success in Japan: adequate distribution and suitable personnel.

In some cases, foreign companies buy access to distribution directly. This means buying up wholesalers or retailers. The most notable cases involve pharmaceutical companies, which over the years have been taking over their former distributors. The cost may not be cheap, but the benefits are substantial since they can now market more of their relatively large range of products more effectively. Indeed, since foreign firms produce so many more drugs than Japanese ones, the distribution network is worth much more to them. Among those which have taken this path is Merck.

However, distribution may not always appear as the direct cause, although it can be an extremely important advantage. In Japan, many manufacturers have their own distribution network or are plugged into one. If they do not have specialized technologies, they may be of marginal interest purely as manufacturers. As a means of reaching the customers, they can be considerably more useful, especially for a Western company that has a broad range of quality products. Obviously, Renault bought into Nissan as an automaker, for its factories, technologies and models. But the fact that Nissan could sell Renault's own cars in Japan, and also Southeast Asia and the United States, made it a far more interesting partner.

Actually, investing in Japanese manufacturers is a questionable proposition, and not one that will always be answered in the affirmative. It makes sense to acquire advanced technologies and unique products, although the price may be high. But for ordinary purposes, to produce standard articles, it may be preferable to shop for a manufacturer in Southeast Asia, Mexico or Eastern Europe, certainly as far as cost is concerned.

The other major problem of doing business in Japan is to build up a competent staff of Japanese, especially since the Japanese strongly prefer working for Japanese than for foreign firms, and creating a complete structure can take decades. Through acquisition such a staff can be obtained, employees working at all the various tasks, from top to bottom, and also people of all ages in the standard pyramidal structure. It may not be the best possible staff, but it knows how to work together and can place its talents at your service. And this in very short order once the price is paid. This doubtlessly encouraged Merrill Lynch to acquire the entire retail force of Yamaichi.

While there are certain factors which can give M&A transactions an added value, there are others which deprive it of certain attractions which make it so popular in the United States and increasingly Europe. It is not easy to decrease expenses and increase profits by various forms of restructuring and downsizing. It is not easy to sell off loss-making subsidiaries and enhance the profitability of others. As a matter of fact, in Japan it is not even easy to know which ones are making a loss or profit and how much since profitability and methods for measuring it ranked low in the concerns of management. Thus, even when they have tried, Japanese companies could not readily dispose of loss-making subsidiaries, dismiss redundant personnel or even do something relatively simple like consolidate offices and branches. If it was so hard for them, foreigners will probably find it even harder.

One other aspect should not be neglected at the tail end of the recession. Prices for land and property have also fallen sharply, reaching as low as a quarter of the initial level over the early 1990s. This means that many Japanese companies, certainly those which own their own premises and may have extensive land holdings in one form or another, can also play on this factor as land and property prices (and the value of the yen) are more likely to rise than fall further. This is extremely important for foreign companies which need offices and land, whether as a site for new factories, locations for shopping malls or other retail outlets, or branches of banks and brokerages. On the other hand, if not needed, the land and property could eventually be sold off to pay part of the cost of the acquisition. The expected appreciation will be essential in the calculation of whether to buy a Japanese real estate firm, property developer, or even building contractor.

Just what have you bought?

The calculation of cost is already rather treacherous, with the considerable hidden liabilities many companies have. But that can usually be sorted out with careful investigation. The calculation of worth, namely what it is worth to you and not just some abstract buyer, is somewhat more difficult because it is hard to put a financial value on what an experienced staff and dedicated distribution network can do for you. But the trickiest calculation is exactly what you have bought. Worse, it is often a calculation the buyer does not even bother to make.

The buyer has bought, or thinks he has bought, factories, technologies, patents, machinery, depots, shops and stores, all sorts of things that can be put into an account and added up. In fact, what he has bought is only those things at the time of sale. Just a few months or years later, depending on how the buyer (and the bought) react, they can be worth substantially more ... or infinitely less. Alas, it is often easier for the value to decrease, and rapidly, than to grow.

Unless maintained well, the factory will lose value. If the technologies and products are not constantly improved, they will cease being competitive, and no longer be of much value. If the shops and stores do not sell the right products, in the right way, nobody will buy. And so on.

This depends largely on how the staff reacts. If it sees the change in ownership as a plus, if the locals get along well with any foreign managers who are flown in and start giving orders, if new management techniques and financial controls improve profits *and* there are also benefits for the staff, the investment will pay off more rapidly and more substantially. If the opposite happens, if the locals dislike the new management, perhaps because from being at the center the Japanese operation becomes peripheral, with too many key decisions taken elsewhere and by others, if the foreign managers are just there to pass along decisions from the head office and make people work harder, if the rules are not only new but more demanding, let alone "humiliating," and the financial controls have the effect of enhancing profits but not also improving wages and conditions, the staff will become disaffected and the investment can quickly become worth less and sometimes even worthless.

It cannot be said too often, by foreigners as well as the Japanese, who never stop saying it, that the company is the people who run it. This is particularly true in Japan where employees stay for a long time (if not lifetime) with the same company rather than moving about from one to another. If they are not happy, and they have nowhere else to go, they will create infinitely more trouble than employees who can quit and look for something better elsewhere.

This means several things. First, it is essential to send in not only the accountants, to check on the monetary value of the target company, but suitable persons to check on the human value of the company. Just who, I must admit, I do not know. For foreign personnel managers, sociologists or other human resources "experts" will make a mess of things if they do not know Japan and the

Japanese. But they might team up with those who do, perhaps local consultants or employees of any earlier joint or wholly-owned venture.

Secondly, once having found any sore points or serious worries, try to explain to the Japanese staff what will be done to overcome them. This could, among other things, include a temporary ban on firings. Any company which adopts standard American and increasingly European practice, of improving profits through massive layoffs of personnel, will only wreck the Japanese operation. To avoid this it might provide more professional or technical training for generalists who fear they may not fit into a foreign-managed style operation. To check that things are going smoothly, various formal or informal bodies could monitor the degree of satisfaction of the Japanese staff, but also of the foreign managers with that staff, so as to resolve any nascent problems as quickly as possible.

A third, decisive move would be to concede that even if your management style brought you to the top in America, or Europe, or around the world, it may still not work in Japan. The economy and society, despite any superficial similarities, are very different from back home and also from other places where you are doing business. The Japanese are particularly resistant to change, as was noted in the first chapter. It is therefore better to advance slowly and cautiously than to come in with all sorts of "reforms" and "improvements" which would oblige the local staff to change too rapidly and would more likely just get their backs up.

Of course, this should not be overdone. The Japanese staff would be quite happy to continue working as in the past, cleaving to tried and true methods which, among other things, resulted in the various disasters of the 1990s. And, for readily understandable, if not overly commendable reasons, they still prefer working with one another and depending on fellow Japanese to taking orders from foreigners or even trying to figure out what the foreigners want.

Leaving the Japanese staff on its own, or letting it decide how to operate is not a solution. Nor is imposing foreign ways. Something in the middle must be sought. And some of the suggestions in other parts of the book, and especially the chapter on personnel, may help.

The bottom line remains, even if it is not very palatable: if you don't do the right things, acquiring a Japanese company may be the worst business decision you ever made.

7
Negotiating that Deal

On reading many of the popular books on doing business in Japan, and more particularly those on negotiating with the Japanese, you would think this is not the 21st century but the 1850s when Japan was just being opened. You are not a rather ordinary businessman come to sell widgets but Commodore Perry, who has arrived with his "black ships" on these inhospitable shores. And the Japanese are not equally ordinary businessmen out to buy widgets but the Shogun's retainers who hardly know what a foreigner is and certainly do not like dealing with one.

No. This really is the 21st century. By now, most foreigners have some idea of what Japan is all about and they should at least know the ramifications in the widget industry. They are negotiating with Japanese who have not only seen many foreigners, they have probably traveled abroad and quite conceivably know more about your country than you do about theirs. You are not the first foreigner they have dealt with. Indeed, they have dealt with many more foreigners than you with Japanese. And, despite any difficulties, both sides are interested in reaching a deal on widgets.

Keep this in mind when you read the books or see the video tapes that supposedly prepare you to negotiate with those wily Japanese. Don't believe anything too far-fetched or exotic. Don't assume that things will be entirely different (although much will be). And remember that adapting too much to the Japanese can be as perilous, probably more so, than not going far enough.

Know thyself first

Most primers on negotiating start with the Japanese side. I much prefer starting with the foreign side. What *you* do is not only just as important, it will probably be much more decisive. So it does not hurt to examine your position and what the implications are.

First of all, as for any negotiations anywhere, you must consider your product and whether it should appeal to your counterpart. If you have done some market research, you should know whether the product will prove popular or not. You may also know whether the other side wants it badly, or less so, because it has something similar. You might even know whether it needs your product to compete with Japanese rivals.

Depending on this analysis, you can determine whether to make more or less stringent demands regarding price, payments, delivery, protection or proprietary rights, control of third markets, and so on. That is what you do everywhere, so why not in Japan? The only difference is that, in Japan, having the upper hand should be used to the best advantage and not frittered away. Don't assume that we are all in the same boat together and wouldn't it be nice to make things easy for my new partner. The Japanese side would probably not do the same if the situation were reversed.

If it turns out, unfortunately, that your product is not that exceptional, that there are some technical or commercial hitches, that there are competing products in Japan, let alone with your counterpart, you can expect much rougher sailing. You will have to come down on your price, guarantee improved quality and delivery, be less strict on who sells where and so on. You will have much less leverage and not knowing it or not acting on it will only make you look presumptuous and result in longer, more painful negotiations.

Knowing yourself goes a bit further in Japan because of hierarchy. Most foreign businessmen work on the assumption, one that is quite widespread in the West, that both parties are equal and being smaller or larger has little to do with negotiating. It is the product, price, conditions, etc. which count. That does not wash in Japan. (It may not even be entirely true in the West.) Bigger companies are much higher up the social ladder than smaller ones. They can have greater pretensions and expect token concessions for this reason alone. Remember that if you represent a small company. On the other hand, if you are the larger of the two, take advantage of it. Not doing so may assuage your counterpart's worries, but it will not enhance respect in any way.

Going somewhat further toward Japaneseness, it should be noted that sellers and buyers are most definitely not on an equal footing. Sellers, in the Japanese context at least, are lesser beings and they are expected to play up to the buyers. Buyers not only can but do make considerable demands of every sort: quality, delivery, service and price. This being understood, it would be unwise to start with conditions that are already so good they cannot be improved enough to satisfy the buyer, assuming you are the seller. If you are the buyer, once again, you would be unwise to go easy on your counterpart as this might induce contempt more than relief.

These points should be seriously considered before negotiating with the Japanese. The rules are fairly strict and hard to avoid. Moreover, they can play into your hands as well if you know what you are doing. But it is not necessary to go much further in trying to fit in.

Books on doing business in Japan are full of suggestions on how you can become a surrogate Japanese. They explain how you should talk, how you should dress, how you should look at people. They then go on to indicate conversational gambits to show just how much you respect the Japanese nation, the company and its products, how you admire their efforts and achievements. To this is added tips on how to go drinking with them, what cultural or sports events to attend (and report on to your counterparts), and where to eat. But much of this is superfluous and you will not get much more mileage out of altering your external appearance or personality than being yourself.

Not only is it insulting to foreigners to suggest that they should imitate Japanese practices and ape Japanese behavior, it is pointless. No matter how hard they try, they will never pull it off. And it is not at all certain that the Japanese want them to "go native." They usually feel more comfortable with *gaijin* who behave as such. Of course, you should be on your best behavior, you should make the best possible appearance, and you should be agreeable. More than that is not really appropriate.

Indeed, going much further is an insult to the Japanese. It assumes that they will be influenced by your artificial bowing and scraping, your feigned interest in things Japanese, your futile attempts to adapt to them. After all, these are seasoned businessmen who have negotiated numerous deals. They are looking for the best product, delivery and price just like any intelligent businessmen. Your appearance will make some difference, but the quality of your product will be much more decisive. So, do your utmost there and leave cultural fun and games to others.[1]

Give ... and take

Whole books have been written on negotiating with the Japanese.[2] Many include extensive case histories. Not everything they say is useful, but much is. So there is no point in trying to reproduce this in a short essay. Still, it is worthwhile referring to several salient points, including some where the "experts" have gone wrong.

First of all, Japanese negotiations are considerably more formal than in the West, although no more so than in many other Oriental countries. Meetings will be held in fine rooms, sometimes located in a posh hotel. Participants on the Japanese side will turn out dressed for the occasion in a well-cut if sober suit. They will also speak more formally. It would be appropriate for the foreign side to go along with this taste for formality, without overdoing it. Westerners can be more simply dressed but would be unwise to drop their jackets, talk loudly or crack too many jokes. No need to warn the Orientals, they already know.

The negotiating table will not be as long as the one in Versailles, but it will have to be rather long to accommodate the Japanese team which will be fairly numerous. The Japanese participants will be seated according to rank, from top executives to lower-level employees and "bag carriers." You could probably tell them apart anyway thanks to seniority. The older are likely to be the more exalted. Senior members, by the way, may only be around for opening and closing sessions, leaving juniors to conduct actual business. Once a (positive) conclusion has been reached, the chairman or some such will appear to sanction it.

The foreign team will probably be smaller, whether because it is expensive to send people to Japan or because top executives have greater decision-making powers. There is no need to apologize for this or feel uncomfortable. You should only take those who really are needed; bringing more bodies serves little purpose. But you might round out the team with a local advisor or consultant. As much as possible, the foreigners should be seated opposite Japanese of roughly the same rank or function, although it may bemuse the Japanese to see the age gaps.

In addition to formal sessions, there will be much wining and dining, some of it pretty lavish. That is supposed to create a cordial atmosphere and allow participants to meet one another more informally. For the Japanese, who like one-on-one relations, it may be a chance to get to know you. It may also be an opportunity to find out more about you and your prospects. You should also get to know them, and more about them, since informal contacts may produce more useful feedback than formal ones. For that, of course, you must listen more than you talk, a point too often forgotten by Westerners.

During the negotiations, present your proposals as simply and unambiguously as possible. Also provide plenty of written documentation. This is partly for linguistic reasons since many Japanese who cannot speak English fluently can read it. In addition, they have a passion for the printed word. They love to collect facts and figures and if any are missing you can expect questions at the next session.

In answering such questions, and presenting oral or written material, accuracy is another imperative. The Japanese will surely have done their homework and will know whether you are sticking to facts or embroidering. The latter would not be well received and could indispose them toward closer cooperation. By the way, after answering the first barrage of questions, you can expect a second and third.

Whatever happens, don't be intimidated or rattled by the questions. Some are put to obtain necessary information. Others are really intended to soften you up and get you on the defensive so that you will lower your demands. At the same time, don't forget to ask purposeful and probing questions of the Japanese. After all, if they have the right to know that your product is good, you have the right to find out whether they can distribute or manufacture it properly. There has been far too much "overpromising" by trading companies and others to simply assume that they can do all the things they claim.

Alas, as you must know by now, you will receive stilted presenta-
tions from the Japanese plus proposals of a sort. They will be neither
simple, nor unambiguous nor (sometimes) overly precise. The
Japanese tendency toward indirect language, equivocating statements, responses that can be understood in different, even contrary
manners, is already legendary. So it may take you some time to
know just what the other side wants, let alone whether you can
comply with it.

Equally well known is that negotiations may drag on much longer
than elsewhere, whether in the West or the NICs, and appear quite
inconclusive until a decision is finally reached. There are various
reasons for this. Some, but only some, have been explained by the
cross-cultural communicators.

For one, as noted in Chapter 4, the Japanese tend to work in groups
and decisions are only reached after consulting all and sundry. It is
necessary to have everybody on board and this can involve lots of
nemawashi. Since this cannot be done during negotiations, there will
be repeated calls for recess or further invitations for entertainment
(which leaves them free to sort things out). That is legitimate, sort of.
But the delay may also be due to hesitation on the Japanese side.
They may not really want to do the deal and prefer stalling to conceding this. Worse, it may be tactical. Perhaps they do not want to do a
deal with you, but they don't want you to go to another Japanese firm
instead. Thus, the negotiations are kept in limbo.

It is vital to determine what the cause is since your response
should differ. If it is only for *nemawashi* but otherwise things are
proceeding well, give them more time. If they are just stalling
because they don't like the terms, try to draw that out in private
from someone you know fairly well and may talk informally. Then
adjourn and decide whether you can modify your position. If there
really is no hope (and here you will not get much help from
Japanese "friends"), start looking for alternative solutions.

Since delay can mean so many things, don't jump to conclusions.
But don't let the negotiations drag on forever either. How hard you
push for an agreement should depend less on tactics than knowing
yourself. If this deal is very important to you, wait longer and if
need be make concessions. If it is less important, withdraw politely.
If you think you could do well enough with another Japanese
company, get into contact with it. I know, the "experts" will tell

you that it is improper to negotiate with more than one Japanese partner. But you must have a fallback position and that knowledge might hasten the negotiations.

When you finally do reach a deal, you had better confirm very precisely what it is. This is necessary because of the imprecision of the Japanese language which has relatively few ways of saying "no" and countless ways of saying "yes" but meaning something considerably less than that. Ask some questions and get some specifics on how the Japanese intend to fulfill their side of the agreement. If you can get this in writing, so much the better.

More dos and don'ts

There are plenty of other dos and don'ts I could mention. Like don't bore the Japanese with tales of your wife and kids and dog and house in the country and your war record although they are occasionally fascinated by your golfing exploits. Don't slurp your soup but, on the other hand, don't forget to slurp your *soba* as a sign of appreciation. Don't pass food from your chopsticks to somebody else's (that brings bad luck). Don't flirt with the girls serving tea or walk off with the hired hostess at the formal reception. But there are other sources for that.[3]

Rather, I would like to make some comments that are directed against the overall approach of many cross-cultural communicators who hold forth on the subject of negotiating with the Japanese. They have often gone a few steps too far. Instead of merely presenting the Japanese way of doing things, they unjustifiably assume that it is *the* way that things should be done and imply that the best solution for *gaijin* is to adapt.

I disagree. If there is one basic rule about negotiating which should apply in all times and all places it is that it should meet the needs of both sides. It would be terribly foolish of you to let the Japanese have everything their way. If they want to be exceedingly formal, fine. If they want bloated negotiating teams, fine. You don't have to comply. If they want further details on your proposals, fine. Give it to them. If, on the other hand, they present their own proposals or respond to you ambiguously, not fine. Even if it makes the cross-cultural quibblers squirm, you have a right to demand further precision so you know what the situation really is.

In the same vein, it would be silly to swallow the Japanese line, since espoused by more "sensitive" foreign specialists, that the Japanese are not legalistic, contractual folks and thus an informal agreement is adequate. Maybe they are less legalistic with one another. With foreigners, it is quite a different case. According to one keen observer:

> Don't let anybody tell you Japanese don't like contracts. Don't let anybody tell you the Japanese don't read contracts. When you negotiate a contract with a Japanese you had better be sure what you are doing because they will live by every word in that agreement. Japanese are very legal minded when they are dealing with Westerners.[4]

What is somewhat closer to the truth is that the Japanese think less highly of contractual arrangements than Westerners do and they are also more eager to modify them to keep up with realities. In addition, they try to avoid actual litigation for reasons of "face" or other. In their eyes, "mutual discussion" (*hanashiai*) and conciliation are much better ways of settling disputes. Still, it is best to get something on paper. If nothing else, this helps both sides know just what has been agreed. In the event that there should be subsequent conflicts, it does not hurt to have a viable base for legal action.

I agree that legal action should not be a first resort. Indeed, the Japanese are situational and even the most legalistic foreigner must concede that the situation can change. So, if your partners subsequently want a revision, consider whether it is acceptable and, if it helps you less than them, get something in return. You can usually find a compromise. Conciliation is much nicer (and infinitely cheaper) than litigation. No harm in trying it. Not to do so would not only spoil your relationship with the other party, it would make it harder to do business in Japan. Still, if you remain aggrieved, the evidence on your side is strong, and you are not worried by fallout in Japan, call in the lawyers.

By the way, where negotiations are held can be almost as important as how they are conducted. The Japanese love to have *gaijin* come to Japan. It permits them to show off their headquarters and factories, invite participants to posh restaurants and bars, and create a climate which they assume is conducive to their own interests. In addition, they know how expensive it is to stay in a hotel and that the foreigners will eventually get bored and want to return home. This pressure could lead them to conclude a deal faster ... and on less attractive terms. Meanwhile, the Japanese can consult with their experts, engage in all the *nemawashi* they want and determine exactly what sort of compromise is acceptable.

Two can obviously play this game. Why shouldn't the Japanese party make the trip to your head office, be invited to your home (admittedly a second-rate form of entertainment), and run up huge bills at the hotel. They might also come under pressure to hasten the proceedings. Alas, it is not that simple. Japanese are not as weak-kneed as *gaijin*, they will not give in just to reach a quick deal. Worse, they probably do not even have the authority to conclude one and must return home for another round of *nemawashi*. Then you may finally be invited back to Japan to sign the agreement.

One further point. Don't fall for the line, often pushed by supposed "experts," that Japanese negotiators are superlatively sly and subtle. That they are insidiously leading you into a trap that must inevitably result in their victory ... unless you can be equally subtle. Thus, one popular book on Japanese negotiation is subtitled "subtlety and strategy beyond Western logic."[5] The cover is graced with a Japanese businessman dressed as a *ninja* and carrying a briefcase and sword.

Well, some Japanese negotiators are very tricky or devious. But most are reasonably businesslike. After all, they are not surrounding a castle or assassinating an evil lord. They are trying to buy, or sell, or market spark plugs, or corned beef, or perfume. Uppermost in their minds are questions of quality, delivery, price and so on. True, there may be some deviousness involved if they are also calculating whether to go with you or stick with a local supplier, whether to help you or aid a group member, and so on. But most of their decisions are fairly rational.

They may also be fairly predictable if you have done your homework. This means that, rather than poring over the pages of *The Japanese Negotiator* or like books, you have been carefully studying the market so you know how your product compares on quality, delivery and price, so you know who in their group makes what, so you know if this is a tempting offer or one they can take or leave. If they want to take it, you will find them much less "subtle" and much more forthcoming. If they remain "subtle," it may be that the terms are not good enough. That, at least, is not an idea beyond Western logic.

Just two last don'ts while I'm at it. Don't give in to pleas made by Japanese businessmen, and endorsed by fuzzy foreign friends, that you place due emphasis on "human relations" (*ningen kankei*) and "trust" (*shinrai*). The appeal may be genuine. It could just as well be a ploy. What it may mean in practice is that you should make further concessions to reach an agreement. So, if you do give a little, try to get something back in the name of "human relations" and "trust."

And another ploy. Don't believe Japanese businessmen when they insist that you take the first step toward long-standing relations by offering exceptionally good conditions the first time around. They will probably not improve the conditions subsequently. If anything, the tendency is to make them ever stiffer. Moreover, there is absolutely no guarantee that you will have a second or third chance in which to recoup. They may just as well return to Japanese associates or other foreigners dumb enough to fall for the trick.

I say this with some discomfort since I was among the dumb foreigners to be taken in. I was also naive enough to believe most of the nonsense spread by supposed "experts." You should at least be forewarned. Then you can either reject these pleas or, better yet, shape your initial offer to accommodate possible concessions.

Language and body language

There is no question but that Japanese is a very complicated language. It is also a very ambiguous one. So you had better be able to cope with it. The best way is to get first-rate interpreters. There are not as many of those as one would like but they can be obtained, sometimes for an appreciable sum. Whatever the sum, if they do a good job it is worth every yen of it. If you do business frequently with the same company, try to bring along the same interpreter. It takes time to learn the relevant terminology and understand the technicalities of the subject. This consistency tends to reassure your Japanese counterparts as well.

It is definitely preferable to have *your* interpreter rather than one provided by your hosts. You can trust him or her more and you may get useful feedback. It is not only a question of words but how they are expressed and what may lie behind them, something that can be passed on during the recess. The interpreter may also be useful in filling you in on points of etiquette and procedure. But never forget that interpreting is a mere service and, no matter how interesting or charming the interpreter, you should focus attention on your Japanese counterparts at all times, during negotiations or social activities.

The interpreter's task is not an easy one given the complexities of the Japanese language and the ambiguity with which it is frequently used. So do what you can to facilitate it. On your side at least, speak clearly and simply and also keep to the point. Avoid unnecessary verbiage, going off on tangents or muttering. Don't toss in jokes or anecdotes or use colloquialisms that are hard to translate. If you do expect to use technical terms, it does not hurt to indicate them to the interpreter in advance so they can be looked up in a technical dictionary if need be.

You should speak in short but complete sentences. Competent interpreters can go sentence by sentence or in longer segments, so you might ask which is preferred. It may happen that the English (or other language) rendition of the Japanese appears a bit short. That may not be the interpreter's fault. The Japanese spokesman may have added lots of circumlocutions or hemmed and hawed. If, on the other hand, you feel that something is missing or awry, you can ask to have parts repeated. That is only natural.

The following suggestion is somewhat less natural. It might even qualify as "subtlety and strategy beyond Japanese logic." Still, here goes. Your biggest problem is that the Japanese side will be ambiguous, that you will get answers that can be construed as yes or no, that even some technical specifications may be unclear. It is hard to pin the blame for this on the exalted Japanese businessman you are dealing with. But you can pretend that you did not quite get the drift, which you are sure can be traced to linguistic difficulties, and press for more precise answers.

This brings us to the question of speaking Japanese yourself rather than using an interpreter. There are now foreigners with an excellent command of the language and who, under ordinary circumstances, can get along nicely on their own. They could even negotiate deals. But, is it really in their interest? For then they would be stuck with equivocal answers and ambiguous conclusions. They could not really ask for clarification because that would either imply that their Japanese is inadequate or – far more embarrassing – that their opposite number is hard to comprehend. That is why many excellent Japanese speakers still use interpreters.

This being said, it is hard to grasp why some academics and cross-cultural quacks now urge foreign businessmen to study Japanese body language. Much fuss is also being made about nonverbal communication through *haragei* or "stomach language" where one's facial expression and gestures are expected to convey – even more deeply and effectively than words – one's true feelings. Whether this is so is open to question. Usually, it is impossible to read anything on the face of a Japanese interlocutor and the gestures are equally untranslatable. Often supposedly perceptive Japanese have trouble knowing what one another are thinking or expressing and, even in Japan, there has been a tendency to let this worthy tradition die.

Whatever the case, while the Japanese do still use *haragei* to some extent to fill the gaps and lapses in verbal communication, it is quite another matter to recommend that foreigners also apply it. Yet, assorted handbooks focusing on the cultural aspects of negotiating insist on the importance of body language and *haragei*. Well, if you cannot tell exactly what a Japanese is saying when he uses words, how can you – a mere *gaijin* – possibly guess his deeper meaning through facial clues or gestures? You are better off not even trying!

8
Getting Personnel

Many foreigners who have done business in Japan regard finding (and keeping) the right personnel as particularly difficult, perhaps the hardest task of all.[1] There you are, a stranger to this country, and you must assemble a team that will demonstrate ability and dedication so that the new company can grow. That is not easy anywhere. In Japan, you are faced with a different culture, different attitudes toward employment and a different employment system as such. There is also, and one should not hide it, a deep-rooted bias against working for foreign companies, especially if they are also small and new ... which is usually the case at least initially.

To understand the problem, it helps to remember the brief description of lifetime employment in Chapter 4. Japanese companies recruit most of their employees straight from school and keep them until they retire. There is relatively little acquisition of mid-career staff and there are rather few candidates for such posts. In short, aside from the very young and the very old, there is not much choice. There is no labor market as commonly understood in the West or even most of Asia.

Nonetheless, you cannot run even the smallest operation without some staff. With a representative office, you may only need one or two persons. With a joint venture, the requirement could easily exceed a dozen. And if you intend to establish an active subsidiary, you may ultimately want considerably more. How then can you obtain enough staff, let alone a team of competent and committed employees who will hopefully strive for your success?

Recruiting staff

Since you must have some staff somehow, you should naturally tap whatever resources exist. While comparatively limited, there is a small pool of mid-career personnel who can be hired to fill specific slots: accountants, clerical workers, factory workers, technicians, and so on. It is possible to advertise for them in the Japanese media, including English-language dailies which are more likely to produce results if you need linguistic abilities as well. There are also labor exchanges and notices can be posted in local towns if you have factories there.[2]

These turn out candidates. Many of them, you will soon realize, are part of an even smaller contingent of Japanese who willingly seek employment in *gaishi* and have probably already been through one or more. They have linguistic abilities, they usually have skills (indeed, more so than the average employee) and they can usually do the job. What is less certain is whether they will prove particularly loyal. Having left a Japanese firm, and then perhaps one or more foreign firms before coming to you, they may very well move on subsequently. Another problem is cost: they tend to gravitate toward the highest bidder.

There is another category of potential employees consisting largely of older Japanese, either retired or close to retirement age. They are seeking a post-retirement job that is better than what can be expected from their company and hope to find it with a foreign firm. They may well do so. But, if they could not get a good enough offer from their long-term, lifetime employer, they are unlikely to be among the best. They will be less demanding on wages but may have acquired rather few usable and transferable skills.

Repeated experiences with these categories of potential personnel will quickly lead you to the head-hunters and executive recruitment chaps. They are not hard to find and haunt the various chambers of commerce and foreigners' clubs. Actually, they are just as likely to find you. They do have long lists of potential personnel, and some of their candidates are doubtlessly a notch or two above what you have been getting through normal channels. They could conceivably come up with just the sort of people you want.

However, they will probably also be focusing on two categories, somewhat better than those mentioned but not entirely so. Most interesting are Japanese employees of Japanese companies who, since they are still working there, can be assumed to be relatively capable. Alas, given the closed nature of Japanese offices, this will be hard to ascertain. If they do come, they may not be the best. They may not have many specific skills but rather a profound knowledge of how their company works plus excellent connections. The question remains: can this be transferred to your own company and help it?

If such candidates are not available, the head-hunters will quickly turn to the other category of Japanese working for foreign companies. They are certainly more likely to be competent, since that is expected by such employers, and perhaps also more dynamic. They will at least have experience in dealing with *gaishi* if not necessarily the specific skills applicable to your own. But they may not be overly loyal and they could be rather costly. The trouble with both is that you will have to pay top yen to get them ... and they could move on to the next, higher bidder in due course.

About now, you may be susceptible to an argument which has been cropping up with increasing frequency. Why not hire women? Obviously, in the above, I never mentioned the gender of the employees because in the Japanese context they could only have been males. Still, there are lots of women who are dynamic, eager to work and have just as good an education, or so the story goes. Alas, no matter what they say, many of them will still retire rather young, they may have gone to less rigorous schools and studied less useful subjects and, alas, dynamic women will frighten the stodgier men in your office out of their wits.

Here, it is not a question of being a male chauvinist so much as conceding existing Japanese realities. Many of the women who seek jobs will not work out for personal reasons or because of resistance from the male staff. Even if they are first-rate, and many certainly are, they may have to be largely restricted to tasks within the office rather than sent out to deal with customers or suppliers. And there could be friction if they rise through the ranks or waste if they are happy to remain "flowers of the office." This does not mean you should not employ them. It does suggest you do so more cautiously than in the West.

Another alternative, one which is becoming quite fashionable, is to recruit Japanese personnel not in Japan but abroad. They can be sought within the ranks of those pursuing advanced education, whether technical or management. These are often more skilled and versatile candidates; if they have come on their own (rather than being sent by their employer) they should also have more initiative, and they are more likely to blend into a *gaishi* than others. This solution was recommended by P. Reed Maurer, among others, who felt that "a deliberate program to search out these people can provide a cadre of talented middle managers in a relatively short time."[3]

As per usual, no solution is perfect and such staff may be more expensive than others. They may also have expectations that cannot be readily met. On the other hand, they will at least speak the language and could first work in the company's home office before being transferred to Japan, which would acquaint them with the products and personnel practices. Considering the alternatives, this is certainly a more promising option.

Obviously, while mulling over personnel, and figuring out what they are worth, you do have to get some work done. Thank goodness, by now there is a proficient temp industry with many local and some foreign firms (like Manpower) ready and willing to provide clerical, technical and even blue-collar staff on a temporary basis and at competitive rates. These people usually possess more skills since that is what they are selling on the market place. If they are not loyal, that does not really matter since you can phone for another. Not only will they get the work done, they will give you the time to evaluate candidates for regular employment rather than rushing into decisions which may prove hasty and costly.

However you ultimately do it, and whoever you ultimately hire, it must sadly be concluded that you will probably have a second (or third) rate staff by Japanese standards. You will not get the most able or best educated employees; the team you form will be quite mixed with regard to age, sex and previous experience, and you can only count on limited loyalty. Your operation could not possibly function as smoothly as those of your Japanese rivals. For this, you will be paying overgenerously. Your costs could easily be 20–30% higher, not counting the fact that employees may put in less overtime and insist on more perks and longer vacations.

Borrowing and growing staff

Given the unusual difficulty in recruiting staff, you may be receptive to an offer from a joint venture partner that it loan the necessary staff. After all, it has its own competent, loyal people who can be seconded to your joint operation under the *shukko shain* system. This will be a real team, with real executives, specialists and general staff. They will be able to function from the word go. They will also be paid the standard wage, much cheaper than a group of mercenaries.

This offer of "borrowing" staff has definite advantages. And it should not be rejected without carefully considering the alternatives. Can you really recruit a better, more effective and cheaper team on your own? Probably not.

But that does not mean that there are only pluses. One drawback is that your partner is unlikely to offer you the pick of the parent company's personnel. You will probably be getting less trained or experienced specialists, generalists who show less talent, and among the top executives some it wanted to get rid of anyway. As Thomas J. Nevins, a specialist on personnel, says: "No firm will loan you their best employees and chances are they are even one or two grades below average."[4] So, even if they are not paid more than other Japanese, if they are under-average performers wages would still be on the high side.

However, all this pales compared to the real problem. These are employees who have worked their way up through the Japanese company, who may eventually return there, and who at any rate have considerable loyalty to it. If they form a complete team, aside from one or two foreigners, they will stick to their old ways rather than learn yours. They will be committed to the success of the joint venture as long as it remains joint. However, if one day the partnership should dissolve, they will stick to the Japanese side and you will be left without a staff.

This means that, if you accept the option, you must make every effort to obtain the best possible personnel. You must insist on careful screening of those being transferred and the right to reject some of them later on if they do not work out. More important, you should participate in the decision-making to see if the managers are capable and have the same vision of the joint company. You cannot pick your counterpart, that is the prerogative of the Japanese side, so at least ensure that you have people you can work with at lower levels.

The third alternative to recruiting or borrowing staff is to grow it Japanese-style. That means taking in a new class of employees fresh from school each year. This method can be adopted both in joint ventures and wholly owned subsidiaries. In both cases, the newcomers will be trained by existing employees and will gradually move up over a period of many, many years as the older retire and are replaced by the home-grown lot. While referred to as an alternative, it is actually more of a complement to both since it takes thirty years to go through the whole process.

There are several notable advantages to this approach. The biggest, in Japanese eyes, is loyalty. These are personnel who expect to stay with the company throughout their career and are naturally dependent on its success. They will fight harder to make it succeed. They will also enter without preconceived notions of how a company should be run (hardly the case for mid-career or seconded staff) and could thus be more readily shaped. They will also eventually form a more homogenous team.

That is not to say that there are no disadvantages. The worst is temporary. It will be extremely difficult to create a proper interface between the fresh recruits and the older staff, whether hired individually or taken en masse from your partner. They will not have quite the same goals. They will not function in quite the same manner. And they may not even have the same pay and conditions. There could eventually be friction or jealousy among the older staffers who fear earlier than anticipated replacement.

The other headache, of course, is that it is not so easy to recruit graduates fresh out of school. You must first approach the school and convince the appropriate authorities or specific professors that your company is indeed a worthy employer, that it will treat whoever it recruits properly and, stickiest, that it is likely to be around during their career and well beyond. Even then, in the early years, you will only get relatively few candidates and they may not be the very best. Only gradually, as you become better known and those you already recruited begin recommending and persuading their juniors, will you get the sort of personnel you want.

Nonetheless, the general consensus among foreign managers with extensive experience in Japan is that this is the way to go. It may not be a feasible path at first. But somewhere along the line, if not company-wide than at least in bits and snatches, it is wisest to begin growing your own staff.

Sizing up the Japanese

Whether you recruit them, borrow them or grow them, you will have to pick and choose among possible candidates. You will not only have to hire Japanese, you will have to hire the right ones. That is not easy for anyone, including other Japanese. It is particularly difficult for *gaijin*, only partly because they are unfamiliar with the culture and find it hard to evaluate individuals. That is not surprising. Japanese candidates are extremely good at selling themselves; they adapt to what they think you want almost chameleon-like and do their best to please.

So, you may be tempted to leave the selection to your Japanese colleagues. Certainly, they have a better feel for what their compatriots really think and seek and how they are likely to perform. They know what is on the market and how to separate the wheat from the chaff, or whatever. Alas, what they want may not be exactly what you want. And they may be moved by preconceived notions and biases that blind them to hidden virtues (at least in your eyes).

The best example is academic background, the primary screen most often. Japanese companies look for credentials, i.e. did the person graduate from a first, second or third-rate college? Did he come from prestigious Tokyo University, or more independent Keio and Waseda which turned out generations of business leaders, or some smaller or provincial school? They would tend, all things being equal, to pick someone from the better school even if his or her ability and knowledge were less. That is pure snobbishness in most cases. The person from the lesser school may be better and may also have to outperform to prove it.

But it is not just to show that you are not a snob that you may accept the lesser candidate. You cannot get people from top schools anyway and, if they do come, there may be something wrong with them. If the rest of your staff does not boast equivalent credentials, there is bound to be social friction. More important, if you are counting on academic credentials to succeed, you are destined to lose because you can never match larger Japanese companies. So, you have to look for something else.

One of the best things to look for is competence. Most Japanese candidates inducted into larger companies are pure generalists. In fact, too much specialization hurts their chances. With a smaller company, and less room for generalists to rise, you could do with more specialization. You also want people who think as opposed to having social graces. If they are a bit more dynamic, that does not hurt. Elsewhere, they would stand out like the proverbial nail that (in Japan at least) has to be hammered in. In a partly foreign venture, that will be noticed less.

Evaluating such people will not be simple. As noted, many of the mid-career types will have left (or lost?) their job with a Japanese company and perhaps moved from one foreign company to another. You have to figure out why. Are they incompetents, who just could not do the job? Are they malcontents, who could not stay put? Or are they talented individuals whose skills were not being rewarded? Did they just get tired of the stuffy atmosphere of Japanese companies and seek other opportunities? In another vein, are they here for the money or the challenge?

If you can reach beyond the "facts" to the motivation, you may be able to recruit some promising personnel. They will still not be the kind that Japanese companies feel comfortable with. But they will be more at home with a *gaishi* and could make a useful contribution, more useful than your standard Japanese *sarariman*.

Your choice is further complicated by the tendency of some Japanese seeking employment with foreign companies to adopt a "foreign" manner. They shake hands vigorously, use first names and speak more loudly. They may also express admiration of your native country, recount their visits there, and praise your efforts at whatever you happen to be doing. The young ladies also have ways of ingratiating themselves. These people are certainly easier to get along with, at least for you. But, how do they relate to other Japanese, more conservative ones who will form the bulk of your staff?

Picking the right personnel is one of the toughest challenges you will face. And the cards are clearly stacked against you. But, even if you cannot get the very best team in the eyes of the Japanese, you can assemble one that is better than most foreign companies. And, if you choose wisely, it will serve you well in competing with Japanese rivals, too.

Japanizing the staff

Strangely enough, despite the exceptional difficulty in finding staff, foreign managers are constantly under pressure to Japanize the staff entirely. This means to replace the expatriates gradually with Japanese counterparts until very few are left, perhaps only the general manager or a shadow chairman. Even they, it is argued, should eventually be replaced by locals. With an entirely Japanese staff, you should do better.

No matter how often I hear this argument, and I hear it more and more, I find it suspect for various reasons. The first is who it emanates from. Although mouthed by docile foreigners, this concept clearly comes from the Japanese personnel of *gaishi* who want to increase their own possibilities of promotion, not only upward but to the very top. Many also feel more comfortable working under fellow Japanese, not least because life would be less complicated. Their views are echoed by Japanese companies which would love to see the *gaijin* go home and leave control to Japanese staff they sense is inferior to their own.

Other objections are more concrete. If it is hard to find a middle-manager, or even a decent secretary, how much more difficult must it be to find an appropriate chief executive officer? He must have a knowledge of the field and the products, he must be able to manage a staff which has been put together from various sources rather than one he grew out of, and he must liaise effectively with the head office. No matter how good he may be at the first two, he will probably have trouble with the third task.

More than that, he may find it difficult to balance the interests of the local staff and the overseas directors. Given the intimacy of Japanese offices, the way employees constantly interact and tighten relations, he is more likely to become the spokesman of the Japanese operation than its master, which is what the head office wants. While this would please the Japanese staff, no company is established for that purpose and this could cause friction which would be negative in the longer term.

The foreign executive will certainly relate less well to the local staff, but he will communicate better with the head office and will perhaps have enough clout there to impose his will when it really matters. He is also more likely to regard the success of the operation, as opposed to the comfort of the staff, as uppermost. He may push them harder. In doing so, he may also ensure the company's success and their continued employment. He should, of course, be sympathetic and understanding. But this should not get in the way of making hard decisions.

Yet more important, whether he is right or wrong in any specific instance, the *gaijin* executive is essential to provide alternatives. Group think is the curse of every Japanese organization, and a foreigner, whatever his views, helps break the mold and seeks original, non-Japanese solutions. This is a vital contribution to a staff which, as we saw, must do things differently to make up for other lacks.

Given the crucial role of top management, Jackson N. Huddleston, Jr. feels that the key post of general manager should go to a foreigner, someone who comes from the company rather than an outside hire and has the backing of the head office. He would be "both the head-office man in Japan and the Japan man in head office." Still, no matter how good he may be, a *gaijin* general manager/president is an alien. There are some things a Japanese can do better. He therefore suggests the possibility of having a Japanese chairman. "This individual would be responsible for enhancing external government, customer, supplier, and university relationships."[5]

The ultimate concern is one that applies to the whole Japanese staff, from a possible CEO down to the lowest level. No matter how hard it is to recruit staff, it is yet harder to discard staff.[6] Even if someone does not work out, indeed, proves to be incompetent, or you must retrench for economic reasons, it will be difficult to fire a person hired on the (tacit) assumption of lifetime employment. Regular employees often form unions and, even if they don't, will be supported by the labor authorities. It may be a long, painful and costly process to get rid of unwanted personnel, one only less daunting than keeping them.

This should not be seen as an objection to Japanization. The principle is excellent and efforts should be made in this direction as soon as possible. But it is necessary to proceed cautiously and be aware of the pitfalls that do exist. You can learn more about that by chatting with experienced Japan hands at the foreign chamber or club. So, even while recruiting, you must consider how to handle dismissals if you don't want to be stuck with lifetime employees you would rather not have.

Laying off staff

During the forty odd years of rapid economic expansion, a crucial task for Japanese managers was to recruit enough personnel. It is only since the recession of the 1990s that they have had to face the problem of cutting back. Judging by the results, they have not been very successful, that is if success is measured by head counts. The reduction in personnel has been nowhere near as drastic in Japan as in the United States, or even Europe. This failure can be seen by foreign managers as an opportunity to show how much better (and tougher) they can be. They may also demonstrate yet again how foolish (and destructive) *gaijin* can be if they do not at least pay attention to form.

Most probably, just like every other manager in Japan, you have considerably more staff than you need. After all, before the recession excess staff was recruited just in case it might be needed. And the personnel structure was never very tight, partly because things were done in groups and not by individuals, and there were no written or even notional job descriptions with specific tasks that had to be done and whose performance could actually be monitored. Within this rather loose structure, there were bound to be countless employees who did not pull their weight and whose loss would in no way hurt the company. But, while tightening up is a must, how to do so remains a problem.

Elsewhere, the first step would be to determine just which employees can be done without. But singling them out already goes against the Japanese group ethic. Since much of the work is done by small groups, it is not that easy even to know just which members are less effective, since all decisions and responsibilities are assumed by the group. Obviously, everyone in the group knows who the weak links are, but they will not necessarily tell. And an attack on the group, or even one or two members, would be rejected by the whole. This means it is necessary to work through the collective management structures, so that each level determines who might be discarded rather than trying to take an almost impossible decision from outside.

Even after identifying those whose contribution is insufficient, there is the problem of what to do about them. Firing is a possibility. And you can fire whoever you want with due cause (assuming you can prove or even find it). But that would not really be recommended either. The labor regulations are rather strict, giving far more possibilities of defensive action than elsewhere. Compensation to the person dismissed can also be much stiffer. And the labor bureaucrats are likely to start meddling in the whole affair, especially if it looks like another case of a greedy foreign company taking unfair advantage of the poor Japanese worker.

But this is nothing compared to the possible reaction of the trade union. On most matters, it is fairly tame, but not on layoffs. The range of weapons is vast, and the most obvious are not the worst. Litigation and strikes are nothing compared to the amount of damage that can be done by passive resistance and "sabotage" of one sort or another. If this is again a supposed case of foreigners exploiting Japanese, the reaction will be much swifter and meaner, with less concern as to what happens to the company. So, for layoffs, it is necessary to get union support or at least tacit consent before and not after any measures are taken. Indeed, every effort must be made to maintain good relations with the union when downsizing is contemplated.

For such reasons, even the Japanese, who know how to manipulate the system better than any foreigner, have themselves avoided such direct methods as firing individuals or broader layoffs. They prefer more indirect, indeed, even devious tactics on occasion.

The standard practice for reducing personnel is not to fire but rather to cease hiring. The personnel which retires normally every year will either not be replaced or only replaced partially and the total workforce will be reduced by attrition. Admittedly, this is slow, only a few percent a year. But it causes no serious rifts within the company. It does have other serious drawbacks in addition to being slow. Due to seniority pay, the older staff is earning much more than new recruits, so the savings in money terms are not even a few percent. Moreover, the older employees are often less eager and dynamic and also less attuned to modern technologies and the whole company can become topheavy.

So there is a case to be made for lopping off the deadest of the dead wood at the top. Even the Japanese realize this and have developed means to the desired end. Early retirement can be offered, usually accompanied by generous compensation for accepting it, and presented on the understanding that it would be unwise to hold out since the compensation could just as well decrease the longer the company has to wait. Those who do not get the message are sometimes transferred to a remote branch office, far away from home and without special allowances to bring the family or even visit it. Naturally, all chances of promotion vanish. Others are kept in the head office, but given a desk in the corner, with no responsibilities or underlings, and treated pretty much as if they did not exist. They are called the "windowsill tribe" since they spend most of their time gazing out the window. Few Japanese can stand such treatment and most voluntarily retire.

In many cases employees are simply transferred from the parent company to one of the many suppliers and distributors. This way they are not without a job, although the new one usually pays far less and may again be rather remote. But that is not the problem of the parent company, which has effectively reduced its own personnel and wage bill. It is a problem for the suppliers and distributors, however, and they may react by passing along their own staff to firms beneath them. Within the *keiretsu*, the possibilities are manifold.

If they are still not adequate, the company may actually create special subsidiaries, the main purpose of which is to house redundant employees. This can be a real company, providing a real service such as maintenance or transport, but could just as well be a fast-food outlet or bowling alley. This subsidiary might then be spun off and left on its own thereby relieving the parent company of any obligations towards the erstwhile staff.

It hardly need to mentioned, since it is so natural to the system, that the personnel cutbacks affect women more than men. It becomes much harder for female graduates to be recruited to the relatively fewer openings. Within companies, the Office Ladies whose functions are less essential are the first to be dispensed with since few managers have the sense to keep them on but have them accomplish something useful. Even in the factories preference is given to men, and if anyone has to go it is more likely to be female employees who are urged to return home and raise a family. Since few enough have risen to management positions, weeding them out is rarely necessary.

While the company is being downsized, further savings can be made by reducing the burden of wages, bonuses and perks. The first to go are usually some of the perks, meaning that management can entertain less frequently and in less expensive locations. There would also be fewer trips abroad, and gifts to clients, etc. might be cheaper. Bonuses are the next to be reduced since they are, in theory at least, not obligatory and a function of business conditions. But it is hard to cut them back substantially and the savings have been modest. The best place for savings is within the basic wages. But again, there is resistance from the employees, and since the employees to some extent determine the size of wages, they have not accepted drastic reductions except in dramatic situations. Thus, even during the late 1990s, the wage burden kept rising in money terms and also in relative terms, being a larger share of earnings since the earnings were so depressed.

Some Westerners may find that these methods are really not much kinder then openly firing incompetent or superfluous staff, but that is the way it is done. And, since it does require a rather special mindset and certain finesse, it would be best to leave this sort of thing to the Japanese partner in joint ventures and acquisitions or at least to Japanese personnel chiefs in companies dominated by foreign firms. What more a *gaijin* can do in a traditional Japanese personnel system is uncertain.

To get an edge the foreign company must do something else. One thing it should do, before setting up shop, is to check whether any prospective Japanese partner has slimmed down the staff adequately so that there are relatively few problems to be expected. In the case of a merger or acquisition, the responsibility for continuing to decrease personnel costs should be imposed on the target company so that the acquirer is not stuck with a personnel liability along with any financial liabilities. This applies where foreign companies tie up with existing Japanese ones.

For wholly-owned subsidiaries, which are starting more or less from scratch, this is an additional reason to create a personnel structure that is, if not quite Western, at least somewhat more rational. With employees who are hired for specific jobs, at least it is possible to evaluate their performance and decide which ones are pulling their weight. It is also feasible to train them for another specific task where more personnel is needed, and thus transfer them within the company. Hiring as a function of needs, rather than just hiring in annual batches, has the further advantage of not creating as bloated a staff to begin with.

9
Distribution

Distribution seems to be a headache everywhere, but rarely more so than in Japan, at least among the more liberal economies. It is certainly much harder than selling goods in the United States, an uncommonly open and transparent market, and even more difficult than operating in Europe or parts of East Asia. Indeed, the complexities have often appeared so formidable that distribution was branded a nontariff barrier.[1]

The most obvious problem, and one that is painfully evident even to the Japanese, is that the distribution system is oversized. In Japan, there are almost twice as many retailers per 1,000 persons as in the United States. There are also three times as many wholesalers per retailer. The differentials are not as extreme for Europe or elsewhere, although they remain substantial. Not only are there many distributors, you may have to pass through several layers before reaching the consumer.

This makes the system unwieldy. It also makes it costly. One reason is that goods are carried in small amounts and delivered on short deadlines, precluding many economies of scale or savings on transportation. They also have to be stored in strategically placed warehouses, another unwanted expense. And they can be readily returned by the retailers. To this must be added the margin imposed for these services by each of the many agents goods pass through. No wonder prices are so high!

These are problems faced by all producers, foreign and domestic. But this is a system that places a premium on long-standing relations. Once in the market, it is easier to hang on and harder to be ejected. Newcomers, on the other hand, often have to wait for an opening and then pay dearly for the privilege of being carried, in terms of commissions, rebates, etc. So, while not actually biased against foreigners, it does discriminate against newcomers, which most foreigners tend to be.

It is also manipulated by insiders. This is often attributed to the supposed affection for long-standing relations and respect for the long-time important customer (*otokuisan*). You know, "My father sold his father's goods, now I sell his goods. We are used to doing business together." More likely reasons are that the supplier has some control over the distributor, through shareholding, placing employees on the staff, financing, etc. In the worst case, they are part of the same *keiretsu* or the outlets are actually controlled by the manufacturer.

Can the distribution system be regarded as a nontariff barrier and in some way "unfair?" The Japanese say, no. And it is hard to argue that the complexity, cost or even lack of accessibility to newcomers was designed to block foreigners, although this often happens in practice. But the inter-company links are clearly discriminatory and sometimes even illegal under Japan's own legislation.

Be that as it may, you cannot possibly sell in Japan without getting into the distribution network no matter how difficult or impenetrable it may be – or appear. You have to find your own entry point, expand it, improve the terms and conditions, and become more of an insider. As intimated, while doing so you may find some of the difficulties are not as bad as they appeared at first sight. And you should be pleased to discover that reforms and improvements are facilitating your task.

Wholesale and retail channels

Normally, you or your agent will have to enter through the multi-tude of wholesalers (*tonya*). There are almost half-a-million of them, differentiated by level (primary, secondary, tertiary), size (from hundreds of employees to a handful), geographic coverage (specific regions) and product (foodstuffs, machinery, garments, etc.). In your own line, there may be literally hundreds to choose from and you may feel at a loss.[2]

Still, the large number and broad choice have certain advantages and are preferable to the opposite. That is because amongst them you can probably find one or more that suit your purpose and are not already tied to your competitors to the extent that you cannot use them. Obviously, you would tend toward wholesalers that specialized in your sector. The fact that few are truly national does not hurt; after all, you cannot afford national coverage at the outset anyway. Rather, you can try one of the major cities, expand to others, and only gradually push toward the outer prefectures.

If you are a very small company, with only one or two products to market, then you may do well enough with just one wholesaler. If not, you will have to piece together a patchwork of wholesalers to get the coverage you want. In so doing, you must be careful to avoid overlap and thus competition among them. And you will have to deal with primary wholesalers, leaving them to handle the secondary and tertiary wholesalers. If you do have several, quite different products, you may have to do this a second and third time.

Some marketing specialists say the best idea is to use fewer wholesalers so that your business accounts for a larger share of their turnover. They would therefore be more beholden to you and do a better job. On the other hand, argue other specialists, such wholesalers would not be under as much pressure to perform. It would therefore be preferable to spread your business and monitor the results so you know which are best. But, returning to the first specialists, you should not spread it so thin that you have no clout. Once again, the best solution lies somewhere in the middle.

Leaving the wholesalers to deal with the retailers, while limiting your control of the operation, reduces your commitment in time, manpower and funds. For this side of the business is also not as simple as back home. As noted, goods must be supplied to numerous retailers, about a million of those. They range from fairly large (but not of American dimensions) to tiny "mom-and-pop" stores.

These retailers, even the most insignificant, make considerable demands. Goods must be delivered in small quantities since they lack space. Deliveries must be frequent, especially for fresh produce. Quality must be impeccable. And goods can be returned at any time with no questions asked. This can be due to defects or simply that they did not move. In addition, wholesalers are expected to pitch in and sell. They have to provide promotional staff to the retailers, etc. Finally, they sometimes finance the retailers by leaving long payment times or providing special rebates for being a good customer.

Of course, you could try to get rid of the middleman because he is costly and interrupts the flow of information from the customer. But that would not be recommended aside from exceptional cases. You will be stuck with much of the cost and hassle. According to Huddleston, "what makes products so expensive is the marketing, sales, and service costs. But to circumvent the many intermediate costs might be even more expensive."[3] Also, although there is some change, the old saying still holds: "you can't fight the *tonya*." You probably need them much more than they need you.

Still, it is helpful to remember that the retailers are also diversified and some now offer interesting possibilities. Working your way up, there are specialty and convenience stores, most of them quite small and with little interest in or ability to sell foreign goods. Then come the general merchandise stores and superstores (*supa*), an upgraded supermarket of sorts. They do have some interest and handle some imports. On the top, with regard to size and also price, are the department stores (*depato*). These latter sell an increasing amount of imported or otherwise foreign goods. Indeed, they have become a major outlet for trendy, upmarket fashions, cosmetics, goods suitable for gift-giving, and speciality foods.

These department stores, however, are not strictly comparable to most Western ones. While they buy, stock and sell many products on their own, they also lease areas or rooms in which the lessee sells its own goods with its own personnel. This is done in return for rent and/or a commission on sales. This so-called "shop-in-the-shop" has become the preferred solution for many *gaishi*, especially those in the sectors mentioned above. You will encounter all the famous brand names there, from Georges Armani to Calvin Klein.

Capitalizing on change

The older distribution channels have long served as points of entry for foreign products. Unfortunately, as noted, they only absorbed relatively limited amounts. Also, due to costs, they tended to carry more expensive, luxurious goods where higher margins are possible. Indeed, there was a whole category of *hakuraihin* or Western imports with overtones of "luxuries." Now, however, the system is opening up more widely and offering more opportunities for other types of merchandise.[4]

In wholesaling, one interesting phenomenon is the cash-and-carry wholesaler, where local retailers with fewer demands for service and ready cash simply buy what they want. This keeps costs down for the wholesaler, retailers and also imported goods. They may be handled in large enough quantities to justify entry. In retailing, there are more "independent" distributors, even of electronics, cameras and other articles that are usually sold through captive outlets. They, too, have some room for imported goods.

Increasingly, price is becoming a significant consideration for Japanese consumers. Thus, some of the general merchandise, speciality and convenience stores, although not yet the department stores, are stocking up on cheaper goods from nearby countries. This is particularly true for textiles, garments, furniture, household appliances, etc. from "newly industrializing countries." In fact, a chain of NIC Stores opened a while back. While less interested in cheap goods *per se*, the department stores are establishing buying offices abroad so that whatever they do get is cheaper.

Other trends in retailing are even more promising. One is the rapid growth in the number of chain stores. These stores are supplied by central buying agencies which can more readily seek out imported goods which are introduced to broaden their range and enhance their image. Of particular interest are members of large groups, like Seibu and Tokyu, which have whole retailing empires, and which can import in a big way. (See Figure 9.1.) To compete, smaller retailers have been forming joint purchasing operations.

If your product is in the middle-to-low range, and price competitive, these can be useful entry points. They are also relatively accessible. You can make contact with the head office, probably in Tokyo. In many cases, you can even initiate relations back home through the various purchasing offices or Japanese stores located in your own country. While *you* cannot get around the middleman, such big retailers can. Do not count on splitting the difference, though: you won't get a much better price. But you will avoid many complications.

Equally intriguing is the development of certain channels which were once regarded as closed to foreigners or terribly un-Japanese but have since become worthwhile alternatives. There is a tremendous amount of door-to-door selling in Japan. It is labor-intensive, it is costly, it is whatever you like. But, if you cannot sell through

Tokyu Retailing & Distribution Group

Figure 9.1   Tokyu Retailing and Distribution Group

Source: Dodwell Marketing Consultants, *Retail Distribution in Japan, 1988,* p. 217.

wholesalers or retailers controlled by your Japanese rivals, at least you can try this route. It has worked quite nicely for Amway, Max Factor and Elektrolux. *Gaishi* also pioneered more informal networks of part-time sales personnel, usually women, following the "party" route. This has been done by Amco, Shaklee and Tupperware.

Direct marketing has also been used by foreign companies, with considerably more success than initially expected. One good example is Franklin Mint. Even more encouraging are efforts at mail order sales with dozens of foreign catalogs joining the lists. Still, in this endeavor, it is helpful to have a Japanese partner. Thus, Sears has worked with Seibu, Quelle with Matsuzakaya, and Otto with Sumitomo.

The last alternative, just to go out and buy land, build your own store and hire your own staff, was almost out of the question a decade ago. With the cost of land, construction and personnel so high, it is easy to understand why. In addition, large stores were blocked by legislation that was only relaxed in 1994. Now, however, it is a distinct possibility. Toys Я Us was the trailblazer here, opening dozens of huge stores that dwarfed and undercut its local rivals, and winning ever more of the market. Other foreign retailers, usually selling niche products, have followed this lead (although usually out of rented premises). They include Tower Records, HMV and Virgin for music, Blockbuster Video in its sector, L.L. Bean and Eddie Bauer for outdoor goods, Office Depot and Office Max for stationary, Boots the pharmacy chain, and most of the high fashion shops. And now they are being joined by general retailers like France's Carrefour and probably Wal-Mart.

Who should distribute?

Given the complexity of the distribution network, the initial reaction was to leave distribution to a Japanese agent. It could be a *sogo shosha*, a specialized trader, a sole import agent or a wholesaler. This remains by far the preferred path. Still, as has been pointed out repeatedly, there can be disadvantages.

For a start, leaving distribution to your associate allows it to decide on many crucial points, from display and presentation to sales price. It also leaves you with much less feedback. You do not really know how well sales are going, what aspects of the product are liked or disliked by retailers or customers, what you could do to boost sales. You will never even begin building a long-term relationship with those who sell your goods nor will you learn much about changing fads and fashions.

Aside from that, as previously noted, it is hard to determine just how aggressively your agent is promoting you. You do not know whether it has relations with another company that offers similar products, to which it gives preference.[6] You will not have the slightest warning if it asks some related company to design and manufacture similar products, and then dumps you. Should it do so, you will have no contacts with the retailers which had been handling your goods and will have to start from scratch with another distribution network.

These drawbacks will probably lead you to ask somewhere along the line: should we let others distribute for us or should we distribute on our own?

There is no abstract answer to that question. It depends on many things. One is how well your agent has been doing. Maybe there is no cause for complaint. Even if it does not give complete satisfaction, it is far from certain that you can do any better. The Japanese distribution system is inherently complex and costly, and you cannot get around that. Worse, it is riddled with special links and personal relationships that would be very hard to alter. If you go about things the wrong way, you may find that no wholesaler or distributor will want to deal with you.

However, the best way of answering the question is not with a flat "yes" or "no". There are many alternatives and a whole gradation of responses. Each will take you a step further in the direction of doing your own thing and you can stop when you feel a comfortable point has been reached.

For example, while sticking to your old distributor, you can add a presence in Japan. You can staff an office which will follow up the sales effort and also contribute to it. You can have detail men and women who go out to the retailers, get to know them, find out how they like each product and determine what you can do to help sell it. If this is coordinated in advance with the wholesaler, it should not mind and might actually be pleased with the backup.

You can certainly do more advertising and promotion of a general nature. This could consist of an ad campaign or increased availability of point-of-sale material. It could also go as far as sending your staff off to the retailer, to sell your products. After all, no one knows your products better than your own staff nor should be more motivated to sell. While this is not done often in the West, it is a common practice in Japan and many retailers come to expect it.

Given the limited scope of most wholesalers, you may have to add to those you originally chose as you expand sales or move into new regions. It is not easy to determine which ones to pick from afar. Local personnel could do a much better job of evaluating the possibilities and arranging for the right distributors. They could coordinate the efforts of the various wholesalers and avoid possible overlap or competition. They could also more readily determine which ones are doing the best job.

If, after carefully weighing the pros and cons, you do decide that distribution is too important to be left to others, you would now be in a much better position to take charge. If, the other possible scenario, your erstwhile partner failed to treat you properly or simply dropped you, you would find it easier to snap back. Or, and this is the third alternative, you may want to stick to your older distributors with your older products and try to create your own network for new ones.[7]

Whatever the case, since you will probably have to live with Japanese distributors and wholesalers, you should try to deal with them as effectively as possible. P. Reed Maurer, who was earlier responsible for the Japan operations of Eli Lilly and Merck, learned a lot about that. Here are some of his positive suggestions:

Approach wholesalers fully recognizing that they are the single channel to customers. You need them more than they need you. They are able to "push" products through the system.

Concentrate on a select group of wholesalers with wide geographic distribution capabilities.

Devote resources to establishing a "wet" relationship with wholesaler salesmen. They know your customer.

Train wholesaler salesmen with the same intensity you train your own representatives.[8]

Profit versus market share

Before concluding, it is necessary to address one crucial item which, for some odd reason, is usually overlooked even in books on doing business in Japan. Yet, it is the most important thing for any foreign businessman – profit. Many authors seem to assume that the honor of just selling in Japan, of carrying your company's brand to the natives and raising your country's flag on this inhospitable shore should be reward enough. Alas, as we know, it is impossible to remain in business very long without profits. And, if you do not earn a suitable return, the head office will quickly recall you.

Yet, making a profit in Japan is not easy. Worse, unlike most other markets where profit maximization is regarded as a normal purpose of business, in Japan there is a competing goal, namely increasing market share. This superordinate goal creates difficulties not only for Americans or Europeans, it fazes most Asians as well. You must therefore come to terms with the alternatives and decide to which one you want to give higher priority.

The case for profits is fairly straightforward. Your company is making an investment, one of many possible investments, and it wants to earn a reasonable return. By now, it is generally conceded that Japan is a tougher market, it takes longer to turn a profit, and there are certain non-monetary advantages to being there. Still, the head office would find it unacceptable to lower expectations dramatically. The case for market share is that even if you earn less on each unit you can conceivably earn more by selling a large number of units. That is also comprehensible to the head office. Unfortunately, in practice, this usually results in less impressive earnings, at least in earlier stages.

The problem is that while you are striving for profit you are competing with Japanese companies that are avidly seeking market share. This means that each time they lower their margin to boost sales, you must do the same. Then, to keep up, they lower their margin again, and you are forced to tag along. This will continue until some company has clearly gained an edge and quite possibly others have been driven under.

So, the most telling argument of fans of market share is that if you lose too much you will disappear from the market and have no profit. It might be added, since this does not occur to them, that if they cut margins too far there will be no profit, and disappearance will also be the natural outcome. The key to survival, alongside quality, delivery, etc., is thus financing. It is unlikely that your company will have as deep pockets as theirs and, even if it does, being foreign and more intent on profit, it is unlikely to dig as deep.

This means that the best approach is to strike some compromise between the competing goals. You can attempt to expand market share as long as it only involves tolerable reductions in margins but you would avoid what the Japanese call *kato kyoso* or "excessive competition." This may, however, force you to adapt your marketing policy. If you want to maintain margins, you may have to look for a niche and, at least initially, restrict yourself to rather special products. If you want to sell standard products, which appeal to the broad public, it is hard to avoid Japanese-style competition.

This is a decision which must be made consciously. Obviously, the specific products will make a difference. Some by their very nature are geared more to the broad consumer market and are sufficiently undifferentiated for it to be hard to demand a price premium. Others, especially luxury goods, are designed to be sold in smaller quantities. Indeed, with exclusivity the selling point, there is no sense in fighting for market share. Most products fall in between these extremes. Yet, for every product, no matter how ordinary or exclusive, it is possible to combine both approaches, lowering margins a bit to sell more, raising them to boost profit. It is necessary to find the right mix.

Often the choice will not be entirely yours to make. If you are working through an importer or agent, it is quite likely that the goal will be to create a niche which benefits from the uniqueness or "foreignness" of your product. In fact, it may well be absorbed in the category of *hakuraihin*. This makes it feasible to raise prices and achieve quite extraordinary margins. This step may be taken by your agent, especially if it has exclusive rights, with rather little concern for your views. The big question then is who rakes in the profits.

On the other hand, if you are part of a joint venture, it is likely that your partner will be aiming at the broader market. Indeed, you probably chose it because it has considerable marketing clout and can move large quantities of product. It would then want to sell at the lowest possible price to gain a foothold and later expand sales. This urge for expansion may not be a passing phase, it may continue favoring market share over profit in the long run. This could result in smaller profits than a more moderate push would generate.

Only if you run a wholly owned operation can you decide on your own what the mix between profit and market share should be. That is one more reason to think of this particular solution despite the relative simplicity of going through an importer or setting up a joint venture.

10
Keys to Success

Every book on doing business in Japan has a section on what it takes to succeed. This is mine. It includes many of the standard clichés with regard to adapting to the market, quality, service, and delivery. But it adds some items most other writers tend to neglect. It is hard to grasp why. After all, price is a crucial element anywhere, including Japan.[1] And, in Japan, nothing is quite as precious as connections.

Naturally, this section is full of dos and don'ts. It seems there is no end to the demands placed on foreign businessmen. However, remember that local businessmen are also expected to comply and, in a fiercely competitive situation, it would be unwise not to do at least as well, although I do not insist that *gaijin* must invariably perform better than the Japanese to succeed. There is plenty of room in the market for good, acceptable and even fair-to-middling companies along with the superior ones.

Although the demands appear stringent, many of them are not specific to Japan. If anything, they should be part of every company's internal requirements. It would be unwise to let up on quality, service or delivery anywhere, whether in other foreign markets or at home. It is just that expectations are somewhat higher in Japan. If you cannot meet these expectations, or at least make a serious effort to be as good as the rest, perhaps you should write off the Japanese market now and close the book on this page.

Adaptation

It is already rather hackneyed to remind foreign businessmen that Japan is a different place and thus one must adapt products and practices to it. There have been more than enough revelations of bloopers in this respect. For example, Sears trying to sell huge refrigerators to folks with tiny apartments, American automakers refusing to provide right-hand drive or computer makers failing to include *kanji* capabilities. There are plenty more and you will read about them in the press. Let us hope that they do not do an article on you one day.

There are many things to take into consideration. One is obviously the physical size of the average Japanese, considerably smaller than Americans although not that far off from some Europeans and most Asians. There is also the physical size of their living accommodations, not quite a "rabbit hutch" but hardly spacious enough for standard Western household appliances and consumer durables. To this must be added that, since refrigerators are small, processed foods should also come in smaller portions.

Japanese also have different tastes. There are some colors they like more or less than others. There are certain fabrics they fancy more or less. There is also the element of texture, usually neglected in foodstuffs or clothing elsewhere but often decisive for Japanese shoppers. They are also particularly sensitive to odors, another factor frequently overlooked abroad. Aside from that, remember that the voltage may differ, and Japan uses centimeters, not inches. Many more items could be added to the list but should be carefully sought out in connection with your own products.

Another more general point is that the Japanese lavish more energy on packaging than most. That is particularly important since so many items are bought as gifts. This can involve an abundant, even exaggerated use of boxes, paper, ribbons, etc. For some articles, like fruit or candies, each individual unit must be suitably packed and then the whole thing wrapped up to please the purchaser.

Less often mentioned, but no less significant, goods must sometimes be distributed through different channels. Some almost have to pass through the *sogo shosha* first. Others may be sold in department stores, but not by the store itself; you have to run the operation in leased space. With so many captive outlets for household appliances, consumer eletronics, cosmetics, watches, etc., you may have to create your own channels. Whatever is categorized as *hakuraihin* or foreign "luxuries" will get very special treatment, often through a sole agent. Moreover, like it or not, your goods are likely to pass through more hands before reaching the end-user.

Advertising, as you have doubtlessly heard by now, is quite different on the whole. There is much more attention to mood, trying to convey the intrinsic value of the product often with scarcely any mention thereof. Indeed, in some commercials, you don't even see the product. There is scant reference to its function or how it fulfils it. And talk of price – let alone that it is cheaper than the competitor's – is still regarded as off bounds.

There is no need to dwell on this. Just read any article on advertising in Japan and it will tell you, first, that things are different and, secondly, that you had better comply. Should you be so imperious as to insist that what you do back home might work here and the agency will deliver a long lecture on why it cannot work in Japan. In most cases, the Japanese (and assimilated foreign) agencies are right. But not always. And things are changing. So ask for slightly more objective reasons and perhaps try your idea out in a small way somewhere along the line. It may be different; but then, so are you and your product.

There are several other variations on the theme of adapting. For example, you should adapt your payment conditions to local circumstances. Your wholesalers, and their retailers, would like to have as long to pay you as to pay Japanese suppliers. If, on the other hand, you are the purchaser and you are procuring Japanese goods, you should demand standard conditions for that. Since delays in payment may be longer than you are accustomed to, you should probably keep more money in the bank while you are waiting.

Another practice, perhaps even less palatable but unavoidable, is that retailers have the right to return not only goods they regard as defective but those that do not sell. According to Michael Czinkota, a specialist in marketing, returns run two to five times as high as in the United States. Maybe you don't have to accept such extensive return privileges back home. In Japan, you would be wise not to complain and to comply with their wishes … if you want to hold on to your distribution network and clientele. You would be even wiser not to introduce the wrong goods or allow defects to begin with.

Still, given the widespread criticism of *gaishi* for not adapting, it should be noted that some have done rather well at it. Most cosmetics companies tailored products specifically for Japanese tastes. Max Factor already has done that for over half its line. Apple, whose computers were initially user-unfriendly, added *kanji* capabilities, as have most other vendors. Ore-Ida made smaller portions and packages of frozen potatoes because Japanese have smaller appetites and freezers. Coca-Cola actually developed products solely for Japan, including a coffee drink and a health drink. And American automakers have been shipping more cars with right-hand steering.[2]

Quality

You would really have to be living in a cave not to know by now that the Japanese are fanatic about quality. This starts with the manufacturers, who hone their production techniques and quality control to come up with articles having the least defects possible, and then improve on that the next time around. If this is what your competitors are doing, then you had better do the same thing. You had better raise your quality standards to the Japanese level and keep going, because they will continue rising.[3]

This is not just to satisfy what sometimes appears to be an exaggerated urge for perfection. If you do not keep up, you will lose your clientele. This applies especially to makers of parts and components or equipment bought by Japanese manufacturers. They can be terribly exacting with suppliers. You must also please the ordinary consumer, who is more demanding than most Americans, French or whatever. Japanese consumers will not buy visibly defective products. And they will return those which subsequently turn out to be defective (or simply don't work). The retailer will then pass these rejects on to the wholesaler who will present them to you.

By the way, it is not only a question of defects which affect the product's use or functioning. The product may work well enough. But it will still not appeal to those who expect each part to be just right. And many consumers are turned off by cosmetic defects which would pass elsewhere, such as uneven painting, scratches or other blemishes. They may be symptomatic, or so it is reasoned, of deeper, hidden failings.

Obviously, no matter what you do, defects will continue to exist even in the most meticulous operations. But keeping them down, and reducing the number per thousand (or million) will certainly impress Japanese clients. Moreover, keeping them closer to the mean will consolidate relations. One bad lot can spoil the positive impression of a dozen good ones. It demonstrates a lack of regularity that could have unpleasant consequences.

Not as often mentioned, but perfectly self-evident, is that Japan has its own standards. Japan Industrial Standards are very strict, and this can be a first hurdle for foreign makers.[4] They may also be somewhat idiosyncratic. Unlike many others, which simply require that basic parameters be met, they may specify size, position of parts, techniques used and so on. This can go to the point that they are disguised nontariff barriers. Fair or not, logical or not, they must be complied with.

Delivery

The Japanese are also exceedingly strict on delivery. You must get the goods to them on time, exactly at the time indicated. There is no excuse for anything else. Once again, this is already part of the structure. Most companies work on the basis of the just-in-time system and retailers insist on getting products promptly, which means that wholesalers do the same with even greater insistence.

They are not merely being sticklers. There are reasons why the Japanese have to tighten up deadlines. The main cause is the lack of space. Manufacturers simply do not have the space to carry large inventories or parts so they must be delivered to the assembly line as needed. Most retailers have very small stores and even the larger ones have little storage room. They have to replace their inventory almost as the products are sold. Admittedly, they have become overly demanding of late, expecting ever smaller shipments at ever closer deadlines. But there is nothing you can do about it.

Thus, if you want to become a regular supplier to a Japanese manufacturer or maintain good relations with the various distributors, you must adjust to this situation. Since you cannot possibly produce at the same pace as they order goods, you will need more storage space despite the high cost. You will want to be very certain that deliveries from back home arrive on time and, if necessary, air freight goods. You may even consider whether, to avoid any threat of delays, you do not want to produce locally.

Failing to provide prompt and regular delivery could be disastrous, as serious as failing to maintain quality. The Japanese consumer, retailer, wholesaler and/or manufacturer would regard you as an unreliable partner. The next step would normally be to seek a Japanese one which could meet the requirements.

Service

When business consultants are not lecturing you on quality, quality, quality, they are probably clucking: service, service, service. That is another indispensable requirement for doing business in Japan, a country with more such requirements than most. But service sometimes appears even less comprehensible – and attainable – a goal than quality.[5]

Of course, you should supply goods without defects, blemishes, etc. And that happens to be the first aspect of good service for a foreign firm. You should also guarantee prompt and regular delivery. That is a second aspect. But you have to go much further.

As noted, Japanese consumers place more stress on packaging than elsewhere. In fact, they sometimes care more about how a gift is wrapped than what it's worth. Well, this love of appearances spreads to the outlets themselves. The Japanese love to shop in pleasant surroundings, in an environment which leads them to feel that they are indeed very special beings. This involves more luxuriously appointed premises than would be necessary elsewhere. The address should be right, in the correct shopping district for the clientele targeted. Don't skimp on this to save money on rent!

They also enjoy viewing plenty of sales personnel. Customers do not like to wait to be served. Most department stores, and even more so the boutiques, have excess staff hanging around just in case someone should walk in. Most of the time, however, they stand about doing nothing. Repeat. They stand, not sit. And they remain attentive, not chatting, gossiping or reading a magazine, but ready to receive the customer should one appear. Another seemingly unnecessary, or at least doubtful, expense.

This personnel, by the way, is not just anybody. Salesgirls are very carefully chosen to look pleasant but not too attractive, to wear the right clothing (often the company uniform), to appear demure at all times and to bow low in the appropriate fashion to each and every customer. They bow low physically on occasion. Otherwise this demeanor is expressed by using the politest language. The men are similarly selected and schooled, if not quite as subservient. This implies recruiting higher-class personnel than elsewhere, with a better education and social graces than elsewhere, and also more expensive than elsewhere.

And don't think *you* will get off any easier. You may be an executive in a major foreign manufacturer, but if you sell products to the Japanese, as noted, you are at least a rung further down the social ladder than the companies you sell to, whether manufacturers or distributors. You are two rungs beneath the final consumer. If there are complaints, from the customer or consumer, you can expect to be called in to explain. You had better adopt the right demeanor, strike the appropriate posture, and apologize in suitably soothing terms. Don't bother with rational explanations of what happened and how it won't be repeated. Apologize for all you are worth!

By now you must have noticed a repeated refrain. Service costs. It costs in packaging, rent and decoration. It costs in wages. Above all, it costs in time. How can you possibly provide all this extra service and make any money? Well, I will let you in on a secret that most other authors do not seem privy to. You have to charge for it! Calculate all the additional costs and put them in your price. The Japanese do it. Why shouldn't you?

Price

While they are full of advice on quality, delivery and service, most books on doing business in Japan don't bother with the issue of price. Perhaps that is insufficiently academic for the professors. But for businessmen it is crucial (sorry to use that word again). With costs likely to be higher than expected, prices must be set appropriately so you get something for your effort.

The question of pricing is rather complex for foreign companies in Japan because most tend to be at the top or the bottom end. You have the brand name producers, often selling luxury items in special shops or boutiques. Even for more standard products, like clothing or automobiles, it is the up-market products which have done best, whether Dior or BMW. Then come the food specialities: wine from France, chocolate from Switzerland, cheese from Holland. Even the fast-food joints, which would be regarded as quite ordinary back home, have a deeper appeal. They all participate in the category of *hakuraihin*.

Well, for foreign imported goods at the top end, normal pricing does not apply. You do not usually price at the same level as local competitors, let alone somewhat lower, but appreciably higher. For many of the articles are brought for their foreignness, which means there is no direct equivalent. Others are luxuries, and as such should command high prices. Indeed, Japanese apparently feel more comfortable paying more since this seems to prove their value. Marking prices down only degrades the image.

Thus, many of the makers and their agents, often sole agents, have done everything they could to enhance the snob appeal of their products. They located sales points in appropriate places, and damn the rent. They laid on sales personnel, and taught it to bow very low indeed. Meanwhile, they jacked up the prices. The only problem, alas, was that some of the goods seeped in through parallel imports (or outright counterfeits) and undermined the image. Another danger was that Japanese competitors could create their own luxury articles, whether Toyota's stylish Lexus or the *haute couture* of Japanese fashion designers.

Not surprisingly, with high prices, turnover was relatively low and this limited the number of units sold. Still, for some, the combination worked and sales and profits were heartening. To tell the truth, Japan has been a bonanza for many luxury-good makers. But this approach could only work for a select few. The others faced the old dilemma of price versus market share in a more acute form. As Huddleston lucidly comments:

> By using high prices as a marketing mechanism to say that the product is quality, the foreign product's market potential is limited to the very top of the market, whether fountain pens, whiskey, men's suits, beer, or furniture. If a company only wants the premium end of the market, that is fine. The Japanese, though, will buy much more of quality products that are priced competitively and meet a need. If products are not priced competitively, the market will remain extremely limited and soon someone will come in and meet the market need created below this stratosphere.[6]

This dictum has always applied to the other end of the market, the masses of ordinary products which are provided by both advanced and developing countries, but especially the nearby NICs. This includes textiles, garments, furniture, household appliances, small TVs and VCRs, and so on. They obviously sell more on price than anything. And the price must remain low to compete both with goods produced by smaller Japanese companies and those procured through "reverse imports" from Japanese subsidiaries established in the self-same developing countries. If this rule applies for consumer goods, it goes double for parts and equipment sold to manufacturers which may not want to drop their traditional suppliers unless they get a particularly favorable deal.

Still, if the competition is tough, the potential has never been as great ... thanks to the economic slowdown. If the top of the market was doing well during the "bubble" years, when the Japanese had plenty of money to spend, now that they are scrimping and saving a disproportionately large share of their expenditures is going into priceworthy goods. What the 21st century will bring is uncertain, probably a more balanced situation with both ends of the market perking over.

In all this, it is necessary to remember one further element which determines price. That is the yen's exchange rate. When the yen is cheap, it is exceedingly hard for American and European companies to compete, although the possibilities of developing countries, where labor costs are much lower, remain rather good. When the yen becomes dearer, gradually Western goods become more and more price competitive, even to the extent that nearly all but luxury items can sell on price to some extent. The problem is that the yen varies so much. Thus, it is best to get into the market when the yen is low, and hold on even through relatively hard times, until it rises again.

What do you do when the exchange rate is against you? Basically, the same thing as Japanese do. You cut prices to keep competitive in the hope of recouping later on. This policy was finally adopted by some of the American and European automakers, although not all, if they wanted to achieve mass sales. Ford Japan reduced its prices substantially and Rover Japan adopted a "fair play" policy. Other companies which sell on price, in Japan as back home, are the fast-food outlets like McDonald's and Kentucky Fried Chicken, record shops Virgin Megastores, and especially Toys Я Us, all of which are achieving what the Japanese rate highest, namely growing market share. On top of this, they seem to make a decent profit.

Connections

If the illustrious "experts" rarely say anything about price, they almost never mention connections. That is a dirty word and the ways of creating them are not fit material for serious books. Well, dirty or not, connections are vital in Japan. Without them, you cannot get anything done. With them, you can accomplish all sorts of things you thought were impossible. So, what should you do?

There are all sorts of connections, and all degrees thereof, so there can be no systematic approach to this task. But you can very well start by deciding that Japan is an essential market and you are in it for the long haul. You should not only say this. The Japanese have heard that song before. You should prove it by regularly upgrading your operations, Japanizing your personnel, etc. You do not have to go all the way. Still, just being around over the years makes you increasingly part of the scene.

You should also cultivate those long-standing relations they talk about. The best way is to keep providing good quality, delivery, service, etc. so that your counterparts want to do business with you. You should also help them sell your goods, say, by providing more POS material or sending your staff to work in their shops. By offering decent payments terms, perhaps slightly better than necessary, they will be in your debt a bit more.

And don't forget what is politely called "human relations." Cultivate your contacts. Make lots of visits. Visit your suppliers occasionally. Visit your clients frequently, even when it is not necessary. Bring around your CEO or whatever big-shot happens to be in town. That will impress them with the seriousness of the company's interest in Japan and keep him out of the way. Try inviting key persons out for dinner and a drink, to help mellow the relationship.

Then come the gifts, at least twice a year at gift-giving season. There is no harm in tossing in some more. The gifts should not be too luxurious for the occasion, nor too skimpy. Especially not too skimpy. Japanese know down to the yen what a gift is worth, what sort of a gift they are worth, and what gifts others are giving them. In such circumstances, gifts can hardly be regarded as bribes. Nor can sumptuous dinners. They are part of the cost of doing business ... and treated as such by the tax authorities.

The further steps are somewhat trickier. You will need a feel for this to avoid being awkward or even insulting and might best leave it to a Japanese staff member. It is precious to have support in the right places. You might therefore create a council of advisors, or some such, and invite suitable, senior, sociable Japanese to join. They are not chosen for their knowhow so much as their connections, which you hope will become yours. You might even recruit a retired bureaucrat from a ministry with which you have considerable contact.[7] Again, that is not unethical. It is done quite regularly, so much so that it is not easy to come by one.

So much for "human relations." Connections are also more palpable. There is no reason why, should your supplier or wholesaler be in dire financial straits, you should not advance him a reasonable sum. Better yet, buy a share in the company. That demonstrates just how much you respect it. It also gives a you a degree of control. This could be consolidated by your joining the board and perhaps placing loyal employees on their staff.

With *keiretsu* so important and so pervasive, you should decide whether to tie up with one. This can be done through joint ventures, using a member as supplier, or turning to the core bank. If you are a good customer, it might urge other members to do business with you. Of course, you will not become an insider, but you will be less of an outsider than before.

Finally, this being the fashion, you could start creating your own little grouping. This means not doing everything by yourself, which is not the Japanese way to begin with. You can establish separate entities, either under your control or part of a joint venture, to handle your manufacturing, sales or other functions for you. These peripheral bodies would still be dependent on you, but not part of the inner circle nor entitled to the benefits that accrue to a "parent" company.

11

When in Japan, do as the Japanese?

There is probably no bit of advice you will hear or read more frequently than that variation on an old theme: "when in Japan, do as the Japanese." You will get it from official sources, you will get it from well-meaning Japanese businessmen, you will get it even at seminars of foreign chambers of commerce. It is mouthed, often parrot-like and without much thought to the matter, by foreign businessmen themselves, especially those who do not practice what they preach.

On the face of it, it makes sense. After all, Japan is a very different country from your own, the business climate in particular is quite different, companies function in different ways and the management system operates differently. More broadly, the place has a different language, culture and customs. Doing things the way you did back home hardly seems reasonable. Not only that, from everything you have heard it has almost guaranteed failure for those foolish enough to attempt it.

But that does not prove that you should do as the Japanese. It only means that you should adapt to Japan, perhaps doing some things like the Japanese but not necessarily everything. There may be certain things that you can do better because practices in your home country are more advanced or more efficient. Why scrap them?

Moreover, even if you try to do like the Japanese in all respects, you will not succeed. You cannot. The simple fact of the matter is that *you are not Japanese*. You can hire as many Japanese personnel as you want, adopt as many Japanese practices as you want, and you will still not be Japanese. Your company will still have some *gaijin* on the staff. It will still have to respond to the head office abroad. It will still be selling products generated by a foreign entity. And it will still have to succeed in the way evaluated most highly there, namely by producing a good bottom line. More about this later.

The most conclusive reason for not falling into the trap of unthinkingly doing as the Japanese is that you will never be as good at it as the Japanese. You are a relative newcomer, unless you've been around for several decades (and even then you are hardly an insider). You don't have a staff you have grown but one acquired in various ways; you don't have solid links to other companies and useful connections to get business; you don't have any government backing to speak of. If you try to out-Japanese the Japanese, you are bound to fail. The Japanese know that perfectly well. May be that's why they want you to try.

No, if you hope to succeed in Japan, you had better accept the fact that you are a *gaishi* and determine what advantages can be derived from that status. As you will see, they are fairly extensive and certainly more than is commonly conceded. They have been the secret weapon of many foreign firms and can help your own. If anything, this foreign dimension can explain considerably more successes than can "doing as the Japanese."

But, you are not Japanese!

Don't be lulled into the illusion that, just because you have an office in Tokyo and your unmistakably foreign name is followed by a K.K., you are a Japanese company. You certainly are under the law. And you will be dealt with as such by the tax authorities. But, to most of your clients, suppliers and distributors, the officials you deal with, and even your own personnel, you are still pretty foreign.

Nowhere is this more evident than in the staffing of your company and the management style adopted. The average *gaishi* has a mixed staff. This can range anywhere from a band of expatriates plus assorted local secretaries and salesmen to just one foreign executive or advisor working with the Japanese. It may even reach the point where the boss is Japanese and there are no foreigners present physically. Yet, unless the company has been around an unusually long time, there will be some personnel who entered in mid-career and others who joined directly after graduation.

Until the whole staff has been recruited at entry level and trained up to the top executive, this mixed structure will persist and it will be hard to apply the supposedly "typical" management system. That is, everybody rising gradually, attaining higher ranks as much (if not more) through seniority than ability, reaching decisions from the bottom up, tackling assignments in groups, and so on. This would be true Japanization, as opposed to the much more limited and superficial Japanization of merely having only Japanese faces.

Yet, before deciding this is the goal, one should seriously consider whether it is worth the effort. The assumption must be that Japanese-style management actually is superior to any other conceivable form of management. As already pointed out, it is very efficient in the factory, but rather poor in the office, where it can be dreadfully slow and unimaginative. Moreover, once the local operation goes over to Japanese-style consensus management, it will increase the gap and friction with the head office, which operates on another basis.

Even if you can "Japanize" on the quick through the expedient of hiring more Japanese personnel, do not forget that – in the eyes of other Japanese – these will probably be "second-rate" personnel. That means they will come from lesser colleges or high schools, they will have had poorer grades there, they will accept the somewhat demeaning status of working for foreigners, and so on. That may not matter much to you. Indeed, you may find such a team not only easier to work with but more dynamic. But they will find it harder to do business with other Japanese companies which look down on them somewhat and regard them as pushy.

Anyway, to become part of the Japanese establishment, it takes more than Japanese staff. You must win acceptance from other Japanese companies. You must become a regular supplier or client, and this can take a very long time. It will also be inhibited by not belonging to one of their groups, be it a *keiretsu* or looser. If you enter a joint venture or cozy up to a bank, that may help. But you will be in one of the outer circles quite far from the center.

As for the bureaucrats, who really count as opposed to the politicians, they also take an inordinately long time to recognize the existence of foreign companies, let alone warm up to them. Thank goodness officials are no longer as adamant about keeping foreign companies down and there is less they can do to boost local ones. Still, you must avidly curry favor to obtain not superior but equal treatment.

Wanting to become an insider or semi-insider is a worthy ambition, but it will not be easy to achieve. And, as long as your head office lies abroad, you will never be quite like the others. After all, the head office provides most of the products even if you adapt them or develop some on your own. It decides how much R&D money will be spent and what gets the highest priority. It may even have specific ideas on how to market products, naturally preferring those which succeeded back home. There is a limit to how much you can impose on the head office and any flexibility in Japan will be restricted.

The most important aspect relates to profitability. You can argue as long as you want that the Japanese are more intent on market share, that market share does count for something here and that it can ultimately improve the bottom line. The head office is probably not willing to wait that long and will want more profits faster. That has implications of all sorts: not only how you price your products but also how you market them, whether you advertise or not, how much personnel you hire, how big an office you have, whether you manufacture and do R&D locally, etc.

By now you must have gotten the message. A *gaishi* is not a Japanese company by some legal formality or even by hiring Japanese. It will only be so superficially until it has been thoroughly acclimatized. And, even then, there will be residuals of foreignness. So, and this is the next message, if you are going to remain foreign, at least take advantage of your foreignness.

The idea edge

There is presently much criticism of Western companies for adopting a "not-invented-here" mentality and failing to realize the strengths of Japanese industry. That criticism is doubtlessly warranted. But it tends to cover over equally justifiable criticism of the Japanese, who have their own form of the "not-invented-here" syndrome. This is especially true now that they have become leaders in many sectors. This tends to blind them to the existence of other products which they do not produce, which they may not even care to produce because nobody else in Japan has bothered doing so. A recent survey showed that it is easier to launch a research project if similar work is being done by another Japanese firm than if it were being done abroad.

It is equally evident that now that the Japanese have pulled ahead in many sectors they have also become more arrogant about what to produce and how. This leads them to overlook many lesser products. Some of these are admittedly niche products, not terribly interesting for big companies but enough to satisfy smaller ones. Yet, some of these niches could expand massively and Japanese vanity will broaden the windows of opportunity for others.

The Japanese also lose through the tendency to focus on relatively few products at a time, giving each a major push. That is the essence of targeting.[1] However, targeting some products implies by definition overlooking or paying insufficient heed to others. Foreign businessmen should thus carefully examine Japan's priorities not only to see what will be tomorrow's winners but also where the Japanese may be losers since they cannot do everything at once.

It is not only specific products that are neglected, whole sectors get short shrift. Most of the targeting has been of industrial products, especially those that can be mass produced. Others, requiring more intricate handwork or produced in smaller runs, may not be as competitive. In other sectors, the Japanese are often poor competitors. Not only with regard to agriculture but also processed foods. The same applies to many services, from more sophisticated leasing or factoring to quite ordinary leisure or fast-food outlets. Regulated sectors have also tended to lag as companies could survive without developing new or improved products, as for insurance, consumer finance, fund management, etc. Finally, there are areas where imagination and creativity have distinct merits, such as software and leisure.

Just as serious as the "not-invented-here" syndrome is the "it-cannot-be-done-in-Japan" syndrome. This is extremely widespread, once again reinforced by the group think and increasing arrogance of Japanese businessmen. Any *gaijin* working in Japan will encounter it time and again. He will come up with a brilliant idea, or simply suggest that the Japan office copy what is done at home, and get the same stubborn reply. "It cannot be done in Japan. Maybe it can be done elsewhere, but it cannot be done in Japan."

Why?, he may ask. If he expects a rational answer, giving detailed explanations of what conditions prevent its success, let alone case histories where it has failed to work in Japan, he will be disappointed. The explanation is always the same. "It has never been done in Japan." It cannot succeed because it has never been done. ...

If you run a Japanese-style office, you will have to leave it at that. But, if you have managed to influence it, to make it more flexible and open, you may be able to actually try the idea out. Don't assume it will work in Japan just because it worked abroad. It may not. On the other hand, it just may.[2]

There are countless examples of products which did work, from Band-Aids to Pampers. Of services which caught on, from temps to fast foods. Even of techniques, such as direct marketing and mail order catalogs. Just how wrong the "it-cannot-be-done-in-Japan" crowd can be was shown by Thomas Ainley, Jr. of McCann Direct. Direct marketing, now a booming sector, was supposedly impossible because the Japanese like to touch and see products, won't buy from a company they don't know, will not wait to have goods delivered, etc. Worse, Coca-Cola was initially warned it could not use vending machines because the Japanese would not drink directly from a bottle or can, this being too uncouth and unsanitary. Now you cannot go anywhere without finding vending machines ... and Coke.[3]

Finally, and this should not be forgotten, many foreign products succeed quite simply because of their foreignness. For some, the foreignness should perhaps be toned down, especially if they are quite ordinary, run-of-the-mill articles. For others, it should be enhanced. After all, *hakuraihin* have traditionally done well. This does not have to be solely luxury items or upmarket fashion goods. The foreignness of automobiles is a selling point, as is the foreignness of foods and leisure pursuits.

One wrinkle on this, often passed over, is that the foreign business community is itself large enough nowadays for smaller foreign firms to live off it. This includes ventures providing services like translation, advertising, temporary employees, travel, business consulting, etc. While some of these firms are fairly big, such as Manpower and the advertising agencies, others are quite small, often just tiny shops.

The management edge

As I intimated more than once, even if you could replicate the "typical" Japanese management system, it is far from certain whether you should. It has many failings which foreigners tend to miss but are so obvious to Japanese executives that they are urgently calling for reforms. And where do they look for models? The West. They want to get away from pay and promotion by seniority and adopt criteria influenced more by ability and performance. They want to cut down on time-consuming discussions and dispersed decision-making which does generate consensus but also mutual irresponsibility where no one is responsible for blunders (just as no one is rewarded for good ideas).

Foreign companies should still try to adjust their employment structure to benefit from certain advantages of the Japanese system. Indeed, growing a staff rather than recruiting mid-career personnel should be a goal. So should some group work and bottom-up decision-making. But that should be tempered by a degree of reward for those who either work harder or perform better. In a mixed system, this is much easier.

That is how foreign companies can get an edge over local ones. They can stimulate their employees to think more openly and freely of different ways of doing things. They can encourage them to be more imaginative and creative. They can break away more readily from the "not-invented-here" and especially "it-cannot-be-done-in-Japan" syndromes.

Even when a foreign company adopts a specific Japanese technique, it can be modified to reduce any inherent inefficiency. For example, while adopting group action, it can limit the number of group members to those who are directly involved and discard those only vaguely concerned or who one does not wish to slight. Employees could more readily do the work for which they are paid if their jobs were more precisely defined. While it is useful to have decisions coming from the bottom, the process of moving to the top could be expedited, perhaps by requiring fewer approvals. And there is no reason why the boss should not occasionally reach decisions on his own after due consultation.

Foreign companies could certainly do a better job of allocating work, thereby raising the level of competence. While some of the staff should be rotated regularly, that might be a smaller share. More of the posts would be held by professionals, trained to do specialized tasks, such as design or accounting. Others would be kept in specific posts where they show talent or ability, such as sales or R&D. They would, of course, have to be rewarded as well as the generalists. This would surely make them more efficient and professional than many Japanese companies.

While there is plenty of room for improvement with regard to white-collar staff in general, the biggest gains could be in a rational use of women. Nowhere is the waste and futility more evident than locking women into frivolous and sometimes demeaning activities. This applies especially to those who are hired for decorative purposes, to be the "flowers of the office," and who may just run errands or do menial tasks despite a good education and solid ability. Encouraged by foreign managers, and perhaps resisted less by Japanese males who accept to work for a foreign company, they could certainly produce more than their counterparts in Japanese companies.

All of this would make for a much more dynamic team, one that is not bound down by tradition, where younger, keener men and women can contribute more and where older, more experienced ones would appreciate their efforts rather than see it as a slight or threat. This could be the true key to success of the *gaishi*.[4]

With regard to blue-collar workers, there is not that much room for improvement, since the Japanese are past masters at factory productivity. Indeed, the flow of ideas and techniques might be in the other direction, with the foreign company using its Japanese factories as a source of learning for its other operations. This could be a precious aid in enhancing competitiveness back home. The only thing that foreign bosses might impart is a bit more decency in treating ordinary workers and a bit less contempt in treating suppliers and subcontractors, which would not pay off in the short term but could improve long-term relations.

The profit edge

Some of the benefits of foreignness are quite simply related to costs. The most obvious is access to raw materials that are cheaper than in Japan and can thus not only be sold there but further processed to achieve added value. This is an advantage for resource-rich countries, whether advanced or developing. Given the costs of transport and electricity in Japan, there is little point to doing more processing there and such a move would probably only decrease their competitiveness.

More recently, many countries have developed a comparative advantage for labor. Japanese labor costs have risen rapidly, a move only compounded by the appreciation of the yen. By now, Japanese labor costs can be as much as four, five and six times that of countries in East and Southeast Asia.

Admittedly, some of them do not offer the same quality. But do not swallow the standard Japanese gripe about quality. The quality is quite high in many other Asian countries, if not quite at Japanese levels, certainly acceptable in general. And, considering the price differential, even somewhat lesser quality is usually tolerable.

While labor costs are close to Japanese levels in advanced countries, they can also profit from cheap labor elsewhere. They should not be put off by talk of inadequate quality and insistence that the best place to manufacture is Japan. Sometimes it is, for products that must be constantly adapted, delivered quickly or require exceptional quality. Others can just as well be produced offshore. That is proven by the fact that Japanese companies themselves now outsource many components and products.

Costs are one factor in the bottom line. Prices are another. Japanese managers tend to keep prices as low as possible in a competitive situation because they are seeking market share. Often, they keep prices lower than necessary when they could easily get away with somewhat higher ones. That is because they are more likely to be penalized for selling less units than earning less money. Foreign managers, who are taught to keep an eye on margins, often price somewhat higher. They therefore tend to get better profits.

Admittedly, as noted, there is a tradeoff. Higher profits may result in lower market share. Losing too much market share is dangerous, especially in Japan. So foreign managers must remind their head office that the bottom line is not everything. On the other hand, profits have certain advantages the Japanese often ignore. Fatter profits bring higher stock prices and thus lower financing costs. They provide cash to hire more personnel, do more research, launch more products, acquire other companies, and so on.

Whatever the case, *gaishi* have regularly generated bigger profits than Japanese companies. This was shown year after year by MITI's Survey on Foreign-Affiliated Enterprises.[5] Recently, the foreigners achieved an average ratio of ordinary profit to sales of over 7.2% against some 1.2% for the Japanese. What is even more interesting, although based largely on anecdotal evidence, is that apparently foreign companies with multiple overseas operations frequently obtained bigger profits in Japan than elsewhere.

There may be various explanations for this. One is probably that only more successful foreign enterprises managed to hold on in Japan. Another, more relevant, is that they paid much closer attention to the bottom line than their Japanese rivals. They also avoided some of the inefficiencies that plague Japanese companies. However it was done, this shows both that foreign managers must be doing something better than the Japanese and that having an operation in Japan can pay off.

12
What Now?

I don't know how often I have heard this old saw: Japan is a tough market, but once you're inside you've got it made. Unfortunately, it isn't quite that simple. Japan is a tough market. And you can do very nicely there in whatever terms you want, sales, market share, profits. But you've never really "got it made." You have to keep at it all the time. You just cannot lean back and relax because the competition never ceases and, if anything, seems to be intensifying.

That is why there are so many foreign companies which came, apparently succeeded for a while, and then quietly pulled back or disappeared. Some of them could not take the competition. Others decided they were satisfied with a niche, which they cultivated and exploited. Those, however, which reacted properly not only became successes in Japan. They were able to use the increased muscle and savvy to good effect on the home and third markets.

In this connection, it can be useful to think in terms of phases, as T.W. Kang suggested. After the first phase of recruiting personnel, establishing distribution channels and refining quality, service, etc., there comes an even more crucial second phase:

> The second phase – competitor catch-up – is where many Western firms fall down. As the foreign firm establishes a new product or service concept in Japan and its sales start to grow, Japanese competitors soon realize that this sales growth could mean good business for them as well. Because catch-up usually occurs with breathtaking speed, the foreign firm needs to anticipate such a

threat ... a foreign firm must function at the same level of competitiveness the potential Japanese competitors strive for.[1]

Facing the competition

There are a lot of foreign companies which could be regarded as "three-year wonders." They arrived with a strikingly new product, an exceptional marketing strategy or particularly efficient production techniques. They had the best of all advantages, uniqueness. And their product swept the market, claiming a major share and driving back local competitors. The *gaishi* was extremely pleased with its success and the media publicized it widely. It supposedly proved what foreigners could do in Japan.

If you take up the story three years later, you find that the product is no longer doing so well. There are numerous clones on the market, most not quite as good but still eating into market share, some actually better. Local competitors are now producing more efficiently than before, occasionally outpacing the initiator. And they have adopted similar marketing techniques, some earlier eschewed because conventional wisdom proclaimed they could not work in Japan.

There is no end to the list of foreign products that were copied or topped by me-too models. Procter & Gamble was the first into the market with strong detergents and disposable diapers, which were soon not only replicated but improved upon. Coca-Cola quickly encountered cola drinks no one had ever heard of and which could presumably be imbibed while eating unheard of (and sometimes unpronounceable) brands of pizza that capitalized on the success of Domino's. Obviously, no manufacturer was ever safe as the Japanese introduced upgraded versions of radios, televisions, motorcycles, automobiles, computers, and so on. The only consolation is that *gaishi* were not the only target. The Japanese copied from one another just as actively.

No, you simply cannot rest on your laurels. And this is truer today than before. Because this three-year wonder used to be a five-year wonder and even a seven-year wonder shortly after the war. It took the Japanese longer to catch on and catch up before. Now, borrowing products and techniques, whether from other Japanese companies or foreign ones is a standard technique. For some of the bigger companies, like Matsushita and Shiseido, it is almost their stock in trade. That is how Matsushita acquired the nickname "Maneshita" or copy-cat.

The lesson is that, even while launching your product, you have to think about the future ... what will happen in the next few years. You can be certain that your competitors will immediately start trying to match it and, if possible, improve on it in some way. That means you must be doing the same thing so that when their me-too products reach the market, you already have one that is somewhat better. And when they come out with a second generation, you should already have your third. And so on.

Meanwhile, in a more general manner, you must continue refining the competitive factors mentioned before. It is essential to adapt products increasingly to Japanese consumer preferences, making them smaller, thinner or whatever. You have to improve quality all the time. Expedite your delivery as well. And add whatever supplementary service can be mustered. Price, as was noted, will be more important than ever and that may be where you still have some edge over your Japanese rivals.

This is costly, time-consuming and bothersome. You may not want to be drawn into an endless race. Yet, as long as your Japanese competitors continue upgrading their operations, you have to do the same. The payoff can take two forms. One is that you will sell more in Japan and hopefully earn bigger profits as well. The other is that, having measured yourself against the best in Japan, you can take these same products and techniques and apply them with even greater effect elsewhere.

Unfortunately, there are not so many examples of *gaishi* taking advantage of their presence in Japan to improve on local products and then sell them abroad, although there is a noteworthy effort to keep up with the Japanese. Still, it is interesting that Procter & Gamble came out with both an improved detergent and diaper which were used to good effect both in Japan and in the home market.[2] And Xerox used the experience gained with smaller plain paper copiers in Japan to help in America. This may just be the beginning. With Japan now at the leading edge in many sectors, it should increasingly be subject to the indignities of cloning and me-tooing.

That little something extra

Foreigners have no trouble following this argument. Wherever you are, you have to refine quality, service, etc. They tend to gag at the last item on our earlier list, one they might never have included to start with, connections. The Japanese business community is riddled with connections, many we would consider not only superfluous but cumbersome, and some which would be banned as illegal or at least unethical in other countries. There are countless links between producers and distributors, parent companies and subcontractors, sellers and buyers. Relations exist not only between companies that cooperate but competitors, whether through trade associations or cartels.

If a *gaishi* is going to flourish in Japan, it has to fit in with this pattern in some manner. It must accept that "minding your own business" and "arm's length relations" are not the rule here. This means that, at the simplest level, there should be somewhat more socializing, a greater effort to know personally those you are dealing with. In Japanese parlance, a "wet" approach. It also includes participation in activities of business organizations and even friendly clubs of competing companies. Although you might draw the line at anything that would be regarded as illegal back home.

But there is no reason you cannot go further, as the Japanese do, with regard to financial participation in companies which serve you and whose service is particularly important. You may wish to buy equity in your distributors or subcontractors just to make sure the relationship becomes a long-standing one. If not, there is no harm in some gentle persuasion through financial arrangements. If you do gain the upper hand, it should be consolidated by placing loyal employees on the board or in key staff positions.

This may sound a bit strong. But it is the Japanese way. Close relations are not forged purely by sociability and friendship. You need something more. After all, due to rotation, there is so much turnover that staff you patiently cultivated are soon replaced by newcomers. Worse, those in favor of a continuing relationship may be ousted by opponents in a management shakeup. Only with effective financial and personnel ties can you be certain the relationship will endure. And even then you may lose out to others, especially Japanese companies whose ties are firmer.

There is presently much talk about getting Japanese politicians and retired officials to lobby for foreign firms. Apparently, some progress is actually being made and a few big names were signed up. But that is easier said than done for, once having sided with *gaijin*, these figures tend to lose credibility. Much more promising is to cultivate better relations with lower level bureaucrats, those you have to work with on a regular basis. Don't adopt the same "we don't mix with government" or "they are just civil servants" attitude as back home. It could be costly.[3]

Keep growing

Returning to business more or less as usual, it is worthwhile highlighting one aspect that can contribute greatly to success, namely growth. As every foreign businessman knows, the Japanese place tremendous emphasis on growth. As for the choice between profit and market share, many Westerners and some Asians will not share this preference, although the latter will certainly understand it better. There is no intrinsic reason why a company must continue expanding, especially if the process is costly and risky. So, let us first consider some advantages.

The first, most painful, is that if you don't grow you are likely to shrink. After all, despite the slowdown of the 1990s, most Japanese managers are still keen on growth. They want to increase market share and are willing to make sacrifices to achieve that goal. Considering that there is only 100% of market share, if most of your competitors are gaining, you are probably losing. And, even if your prices are higher and your profit margins thicker, you are bound to be hurt on the profit side as well by selling fewer units relatively. If worst comes to worst, and it sometimes does in Japan, you could even be driven out of the market. So you could only neglect chances for growth at your own peril.

Growth will help you with productivity. You have a given staff, offices, factories, warehouses and so on. If you increase sales, you will be enhancing the productivity of these fixed investments. Higher productivity will ultimately help your bottom line. That is one justification for modest growth that any head office can understand. The folks back home will only question further expansion,

expansion that requires more staff, offices, factories, warehouses and so on.

Still, if you are growing yet more rapidly, you can more readily accomplish many of your other goals. With a larger operation, it is much easier to come out with new, improved products, to refine production techniques, to shorten delivery times, etc. Growth, especially among Japanese, also invigorates the staff. Salesmen push ahead more aggressively, managers rally the ranks of *sararimen* and factory workers who, since there may be more overtime or bigger bonuses, are willing to make greater sacrifices.

Growth also ties in with personnel management more intimately if you adopt the Japanese system. If you merely hire and fire, then you can add or discard staff in keeping with production levels. If you bring in new classes of young employees and intend to keep them throughout a career, there must be something for them to do not only now but three decades from now. They should also have legitimate hopes of riding the escalator up. That can only be provided by an expanding operation. Just holding your own is not enough.

This, however, does not mean that you have to succumb to the growth mania that affects many Japanese, where projects are adopted purely for reasons of growth or to keep the staff happy, without considering their merits. Nor do you have to introduce a new model, build a new factory or launch an ambitious advertising campaign just because your competitors do. It is necessary to weigh the pros and cons more soberly than most Japanese managers. You have to determine whether it will yield an acceptable return and, above all, whether your rivals are not all doing the same thing at the same time which could be ruinous.

Moreover, if you want to grow, there are more ways than one. The most obvious is to add new products. There is nothing unusual about that. Yet, as an extension of a foreign company, you may be in a somewhat better position. You may not have to develop these products but simply pick some of those already being sold back home and check whether they can do well in Japan. In fact, given the importance of growth, this should be part of a strategy of starting with one or two especially promising articles and gradually expanding.

Another relatively tame way of growing is to enlarge the distribution network. There are probably dozens of wholesalers and other distributors in your sector and you may just be working with a few. It would not hurt to add more gradually. Obviously, when adding, you should try to avoid duplication by going into new regions or types of outlets. Meanwhile, the older distributors can be satisfied by letting them handle some of the new products added to the line. Or, if you are more ambitious, you might try marketing some of these products yourself.

A further step, this time more audacious, is to take up local production. This can be done in various ways. If you already have a joint venture, the task will be shared with your partner who doubtlessly has more experience and may just suggest using one of its existing plants and personnel. That is easier. But the risk remains that now, in addition to controlling distribution, your partner will know how to manufacture the products. If you have your own operation you may still go into a specific joint venture to manufacture a specific product but choose another associate for the next, so as to dilute the risk.

It is certainly more complicated and costly to set up your own factory from scratch, recruit a completely new staff, train technicians, managers, etc. This is also very risky. You will not know from the outset just how big the plant should be. Too small and it is less productive than those of your competitors. Too large and you will be stuck with excess capacity. You may then fall into the usual trap of cutting prices to boost sales and thereby neglecting profit, which would not appeal to the head office.

A third alternative, one I have seldom heard but sounds very constructive, was suggested by Kuniyasu Sakai, an author *and* businessman. That is to tap into the Japanese subcontracting system: "A foreign company could choose to bypass the big Japanese manufacturer, split up production among a couple of reliable smaller companies, and avoid the whole problem. The key to this approach is the basic interests of the small subcontractor: it doesn't want to compete with you – it wants more orders from you."[4]

The advantages are considerable, some already mentioned. Less risk of being dominated by your partner, less chance of it creating a clone product that ultimately competes against you, yet the ability to have others produce what you need without getting involved in manufacturing yourself. But that is not all. As I noted earlier on, subcontractors tend to be quite efficient, they are much cheaper than large companies and they could become dependent on you. If you do well, they can expand production or you can add more sub-contractors. If things do not work out, you can lay them off.

The final step, the consecration as it were, is local research and development. That will really prove to the Japanese business community and your own employees that you are in for the long haul. That is obviously not why you should make the decision. Far better reasons are that Japan now has a large number of trained and experienced research workers and many advanced technologies originate here. If you want to keep ahead, you should take advantage. That is already being done by IBM, DuPont, Eastman Kodak and many of the pharmaceutical firms.

Upgrade your operation

Growth can assume another dimension as well. This involves raising your profile in Japan and, while so doing, increasing your commitment and chances of success. The path was already marked out rather clearly when referring to the various points of entry. It is possible to enter at one of the lower and subsequently move up.

The lowest rung, as indicated, is merely to export to Japan whether through a trading company or a smaller importer. At this level, however, you are almost entirely dependent on the agent's ability. There is little means of evaluating how effective a job it is doing. There is not much feedback from the customers. You do not even have that much influence over advertising or pricing. Worst of all, you never know when the agent may replace you with another supplier.

With a representative office, you can at least maintain some degree of control. You can more readily check on the efficiency of distribution and evaluate consumer tastes to determine whether and how to modify any product. You can also get a better feel for pricing, advertising and other forms of promotion. Knowing the market better, you may also encounter alternative distribution channels. You could even replace the trading company or importer and take charge of marketing yourself.

Moving to a joint venture or a wholly owned, full-scale operation is a big step. It is probably best to decide from the outset which it will be since forming a joint venture is complicated and costly.

Dissolving one is even more troublesome and, if your old partner is not happy, could leave you with a battered reputation. Worse, the former partner could turn into a competitor. Nonetheless, there has been a definite trend for foreign companies which started out with joint ventures to dissolve them or buy out the Japanese side. This was done by Bayer, Corning and Kodak.

It is only at the level of a joint venture or wholly owned subsidiary that you can seriously think of marketing or manufacturing. Unfortunately, in the former case, your partner – who knows the situation better – is more likely to take the lead and acquire contacts and expertise you would be wise to reserve for yourself. Equally important, your partner will probably control most of the personnel. If the joint venture ever falls apart, you would not be able to salvage much of it.

So, if you do expect eventually to go into active marketing and manufacturing, let alone R&D, it may be best to skip the joint venture stage entirely. On the other hand, if it does ease entry, another alternative may be considered. Rather than tying up with a large partner that could dominate you, try a smaller one that you can dominate or one in an unrelated sector. With the former, you might eventually buy into or even take over the partner and, in the latter, a divorce would be smoother. It might also be possible to acquire smaller distributors or subcontractors which have manufactured goods for you.

Now that acquisitions are becoming just another strategy for expansion, although certainly not as common or easy in Japan as in the West, this option should be seriously considered by acquisitive foreign companies. One way of expanding quickly may be to buy a major Japanese company which has its own subordinate firms and is also part of a broader corporate group, as for Nissan. Another, more cautious way is to expand gradually by taking over one distributor or subcontractor and then another. Since friendly takeovers are much simpler, smoother and more likely to succeed, *gaishi* with a longer exposure to Japan may gradually acquire their former partners and associates. Actually, this may be welcome, since Japanese companies could well prefer becoming part of a larger multinational to being swallowed up by a Japanese rival. That probably explains Isuzu's acceptance of a stake by General Motors and Mazda's increasing absorption in Ford.

These could be individual steps, taken as the opportunities arise, or part of a masterplan to achieve the ultimate goal, the creation of your own group or *keiretsu*. This can go in all three directions, with the parent company controlling suppliers and subcontractors, dominating distributors and even doing business on a reasonably equal footing with a major bank and its related companies. Examples of this are Bayer, BASF, DuPont, Exxon, General Electric and, of course, IBM.[6]

What if it doesn't work out?

The literature on foreign companies operating in Japan is rather one-sided. It tends to stress the successes which were apparently achieved by using the tried-and-true methods espoused by the writer.[7] There were failures, it is admitted, but that is because the *gaishi* did not do things right. It did not adapt its products, it did not refine quality, it did not meet deadlines, it could not cooperate with Japanese distributors or joint venture partners and so on. The solution, the only one most "experts" can conceive of, is to try harder because, as we all know, Japan is a tough market and it takes time.

This whole patter is wrong. First of all, there are more failures than are generally conceded. These failures include not only companies which have publicly given up and pulled out. There are others which still function but cannot cover their costs or even generate enough business to keep their employees busy. Many show reasonable profits. But, if they are losing market share at the same time, their future is hardly assured. Others are comfortable joint ventures where the Japanese partner runs the personnel, sales and production and may ultimately find that a foreign partner is a drag.

No matter how unpleasant it may be, many of the *gaishi* would be wise to admit their failure or at least lack of convincing success. They should then consider which measures can be taken to turn the venture around. In some cases, this may involve rather dramatic reforms, in others, relatively minor changes. What they do will depend very heavily on where the fault lies.

Most often it is simply assumed that the foreign side must be doing something wrong. This may well be. The man sent out by the head office may not be good in a foreign setting, especially the Japanese one. He may not relate well to the personnel or grasp the tricky marketing situation. He may find it hard to cooperate and prefer giving orders. Even more simply, the product chosen to spearhead the entry may have been the wrong one. It sold well in New York, or London, or Singapore, but bombed in Japan, at any rate in its present form.

On the other hand, it may not be the fault of the foreign company but those it is working with in Japan. This sort of possibility arises particularly in the case of exporting or licensing. It is entirely possible that the trader, importer or manufacturer is not terribly efficient. It may not have the best distribution network or, even if it is good, it may not be entirely adapted to the needs of your product. In addition, since it tends to do things its own way, it may not truly understand the product's selling points. If it has an interest in other companies which make competing products or, even more insidious, is controlled by them, it may not be very committed to your success.

In joint ventures, there can be similar problems. The Japanese partner may not have as good a distribution network as was assumed and it may not even be manufacturing as efficiently as others. That can happen. More likely is that the parent company has other things to worry about, projects with a higher priority, and it therefore only transferred to your operation some of its less competent or dynamic people and less efficient production facilities. More serious, once again, it may now be in a position where it could produce and sell a comparable product and would secretly like to see the joint venture collapse.

So, why not consider a failure in Japan as coolly and objectively as anywhere else? Just because you feel you must succeed and just because the media will jump on any setback does not mean you have to continue along the same path. There is no reason you cannot recall the expatriate boss or even depose a Japanese CEO. You could very well try other distributors or even completely different channels. If things are bad enough, you may want to dissolve a joint venture and go out on your own. Less often, but still a possibility, you may find that creating a wholly owned subsidiary was too ambitious and you are better off with a local partner who knows the market and has more clout.

There are drawbacks to all of these solutions. You may have to revamp your whole distribution and even production machinery, you may make enemies with former employees who can have allies within the existing staff, you will certainly anger the distributors, which should not be done lightly. Your former joint venture partner will not be very happy and it can influence others in the group or more broadly. You may end up with a bad reputation. This is all negative, very negative. But it is probably less harmful than preserving an operation that is a failure and continues being a burden on the company and source of ridicule in the Japanese business community.

If worse comes to worst, you may even have to take a decision that is anathema to most consultants ... withdraw from Japan. That is the clearest admission of failure and it is particularly embarrassing in Japan where your fellow *gaijin* will excoriate you and Japanese companies will claim you have proven that foreigners cannot hack it. Yet, no matter how painful the decisions it is better to fail and leave than to fail and stay. You will look less ridiculous and perhaps gradually be forgotten.

Is a comeback possible? Can you revamp, retrench or return? For some odd reason, the consensus is that you cannot. That seems to be based largely on theory and cultural considerations. In practice, companies have failed the first time and yet succeeded the second time around. They seriously considered their weaknesses, plotted a more intelligent strategy and made some of the changes mentioned, like trying other personnel, products, distributors, partners or going it alone. They usually also put greater manpower and finance into the new effort and gave success in Japan a higher priority.

There are examples of this. A major reversal in fortune came for automakers in general as duties and NTBs were eliminated, but also as they switched from use of importers to opening their own dealerships, BMW being the most prominent. General Foods, on the other hand, having failed to expand its market share for instant coffee alone, became more effective in a tie-up with Ajinomoto. Kodak, an old-timer, only really began clicking when it gave Japan the priority it merited while Agfa found its more modest way by selling film under a Daiei private brand. Nothing is more instructive than the already cited experience of Procter & Gamble, whose initial successes with detergents and diapers were undermined by Japanese clones, which it then improved upon. And nothing shows better how much Japan has changed than Renault's sudden rise from a minor to a major player through its deal with Nissan.

Actually, comebacks and turnarounds have been occurring with increasing frequency as the artificial barriers come down and *gaishi* figure out how the market works. This makes any hard-and-fast rules rather questionable. It is a matter of trying, and trying, and trying again until you find the right combination to succeed. If I am not mistaken, that principle applies in most countries, and not only Japan. The only difference is that here you have to try a bit harder.

Notes and References

Chapter 1 A different Japan?

1. To put the economic decline in perspective, see Richard Katz, *Japan: The System That Soured*, and Jon Woronoff, *The Japanese Economic Crisis*.
2. Typical of the literature on this era is Sheridan M. Tatsuno, *Created in Japan*.
3. An extensive sampling of this literature can be found in the bibliography under Japanese Management.
4. For some insight into JETRO's conversion to promoting imports, see Chapter 2, First Things First (section entitled "What to do before you go").

Chapter 2 First things first

1. *Nippon 1998, Business Facts and Figures*, JETRO, Tokyo, 1998, p. 115.
2. On demographic trends and evolving consumer tastes, see George Fields, *Gucci on the Ginza*.
3. *Business America*, September 24, 1990.
4. On the proliferation of small foreign companies, see Helene Thian, *Setting Up & Operating a Business in Japan*.
5. On trade barriers and nontariff barriers, see Michael Czinkota and Jon Woronoff, *Unlocking Japan's Markets*; Clyde V. Prestowitz, *Trading Places*; and Woronoff, *World Trade War*.
6. More details on JETRO publications are provided in the bibliography. Several addresses are indicated in the Directory.
7. For a list, see JETRO's annual *Trade Fairs in Japan*.

Chapter 3 Corporate community

1. For a description of the different types of groupings and their impact on business, see Czinkota and Woronoff, op. cit., pp. 31–74. For membership of the leading groups, see Dodwell, *Industrial Groupings in Japan*. For an analysis of how the *keiretsu* operate, see Kenichi Miyashita and David Russell, *Keiretsu*.
2. Marie Anchordoguy, "A Brief History of Japan's Keiretsu," *Harvard Business Review*, July–August 1990, p. 59.
3. On the role of trade associations, see Leonard H. Lynn and Timothy J. McKeown, *Organizing Business*. For a directory, with specific functions, see JETRO's *Activities of Industrial Organizations in Japan*.
4. For addresses of some foreign chambers, see the Directory.

5. On the government's role in the economy, see Woronoff, *Japanese Targeting*.
6. Mark Zimmerman, *How To Do Business with the Japanese*, pp. 100–1.

Chapter 4   Business-related culture

1. For broader studies of Japanese management you would probably do better to skip the "pop" works of the gurus and scholarly tomes of the foreign academics and try some written by Japanese specialists. Examples are Keitaro Hasegawa, *Japanese-Style Management*; Shuji Hayashi, *Culture and Management in Japan*, Kazuo Koike, *Understanding Industrial Relations in Japan*; and Toyohiro Kono, *Strategy & Structure of Japanese Enterprises*; or also Noboru Yoshimura and Philip Anderson, *Inside the Kaisha*.
2. Even supposedly hard-headed businessmen like James and Jeffrey Morgan wax poetic about loyalty, harmony, etc. in *Cracking the Japanese Market*.
3. There are literally dozens of books on Japanese productivity, quality control and other techniques, most too specialized for the uninitiated. More general books are Masaaki Imai, *Kaizen*; and Sheridan, *Created in Japan*.
4. For further details on the inefficiency of white-collar employees and management in general, see Woronoff, *Japan's Wasted Workers*.
5. The sorry situation of women workers, no better now than then, is described in Janet E. Hunter (ed.), *Japanese Women Working*; and the sheer futility of the OLs appears in Jeannie Lo, *Office Ladies, Factory Women*.

Chapter 5   Choosing the right vehicle

1. For further background on the various vehicles, see Czinkota and Woronoff, op. cit., pp. 141–75.
2. The nine *sogo shosha*, listed by turnover, are C. Itoh, Sumitomo, Mitsubishi, Marubeni, Mitsui, Nissho Iwai, Toyo Menka, Nichimen and Kanematsu-Gosho.
3. To check the links between the general trading companies and the *keiretsu*, see Dodwell, *Industrial Groupings in Japan*.
4. On McDonald's success story, see James L. Watson, *Golden Arches East*.
5. On how this works in the pharmaceutical sector, see Reed Maurer, *Competing in Japan*, pp. 106–24.
6. For practical tips on how joint ventures operate, by executives who participated in them, see Huddleston, op. cit., T.W. Kang, *Gaishi*, Maurer, op. cit., Morgan and Morgan, op. cit., and Zimmerman, op. cit.
7. Huddleston, op. cit., p. 121.
8. Zimmerman, op. cit., p. 232.

9. For some of the nuts and bolts of incorporation, taxation, etc., see Takashi Kuboi, *Business Practices and Taxation in Japan*, and Thian, op. cit.
10. Kang, op. cit., pp. 215–17.

Chapter 6   Mergers and acquisitions

1. *The Economist*, April 3, 1999, pp. 55–6.
2. Ibid., July 19, 1997, p. 73.
3. For details, see Toyo Keizai, *Japan Company Handbook*.
4. The literature on acquisitions is still very sparse, although it is bound to grow. An early study is Kenji Ishizumi, *Acquiring Japanese Companies*.

Chapter 7   Negotiating that deal

1. Thian also suggests being yourself. "The advantage of being foreign is to use your 'foreignness,' meaning that you can be straightforward and get the answers because the Japanese will expect such behavior. Remember not to play either role, the ugly American (or other nationality) or the Japanized foreigner, bowing lower, eating more raw fish, and swigging more *saké* than your Japanese host." Thian, op. cit., p. 27.
2. On negotiating, to be taken sometimes with a grain of salt, see John L. Graham and Yoshihiro Sano, *Smart Bargaining*, Robert M. March, *The Japanese Negotiator*; Robert T. Moran, *Getting Your Yen's Worth*; and Rosalie L. Tung, *Business Negotiations with the Japanese*. On negotiating by a businessman, not an academic, see Zimmerman, op. cit., pp. 91–129.
3. On Japanese business etiquette, to be taken with two grains of salt, see Jon Alston, *The Intelligent Businessman's Guide to Japan*; Boye de Mente, *How To Do Business with the Japanese*; Diana Rowland, *Japanese Business Etiquette*; and James M. Vardaman, Jr. and Michiko Sasaki, *Japanese Etiquette Today*.
4. Huddleston, op. cit., p. 89.
5. *The Japanese Negotiator* by March.

Chapter 8   Getting personnel

1. For interesting comments on the problem of seeking and selecting personnel, from a practical viewpoint, see Kang, op. cit., pp. 117–82, Huddleston, op. cit., pp. 19–69, and Maurer, op. cit., pp. 65–83.
2. For pointers on recruitment techniques, see Thomas J. Nevins, *Labor Pains and the Gaijin Boss* and *Taking Charge in Japan*.
3. Maurer, op. cit., p. 79.
4. Nevins, "Six Strategic Tools for Business Success in Japan," *Journal of the ACCJ*. March 1989, p. 26.

5. Huddleston, op. cit., p. 17. For frank comments on whether to hire expatriates or Japanese for top posts, see also pp. 8–17.
6. On the difficulties of dismissals, see Nevins, *Taking Charge in Japan.*

Chapter 9   Distribution

1. For further background on distribution and marketing, see Erich Batzer and Helmut Laumer, *Marketing Strategies and Distribution Channels for Foreign Companies in Japan*, and Czinkota and Woronoff, op. cit. For practical details, see Dodwell, *Retail Distribution in Japan*, and appropriate JETRO publications including *A Wealth of Opportunity. Japan's Distribution Channels.*
2. For information on wholesalers and retailers, see Dodwell, op. cit., and JETRO's *Japan Trade Directory.*
3. Huddleston, op. cit., p. 180.
4. On changes in the distribution sector, see Czinkota and Woronoff, op. cit., pp. 109–27.
5. Actually, despite initial resistance, direct marketing has been one of the fastest growing sectors.
6. To find the links of some major distributors, see Dodwell, *Industrial Grouping in Japan*. For information on who sells to whom, see Dodwell, *Retail Distribution in Japan.*
7. For an analysis of how several foreign companies tackled their marketing problems, see Huddleston, op. cit., pp. 168–95.
8. Maurer, op. cit., pp. 138–9.

Chapter 10   Keys to success

1. Kang also places special stress on quality, cost/price, delivery and service as the vital factors which he sums up as QCDS. See Kang, op. cit., pp. 2–17.
2. More examples can be found in Robert C. Christopher, *Second to None.*
3. On Japanese concern with quality and product upgrading, see Imai, op. cit., and Tatsuno, op. cit.
4. For further information on Japanese standards, contact JETRO which can direct you to the pertinent standard-setting bodies and has translated many of the most useful standards into English.
5. On the peculiar demands of service, see Robert M. March, *Honoring the Customer*, and Chuck Loughlin and Karen Sage, *Samurai Selling.*
6. Huddleston, op. cit., p. 195.
7. For comments on relations with the bureaucracy, see Huddleston, op. cit., pp. 94–107. On the more recent weakening of links, see Frank Gibney (ed.), *Unlocking the Bureaucratic Kingdom.*

Chapter 11 When in Japan, do as the Japanese?

1. On Japanese targeting, what it involves and which sectors were picked see Woronoff, *Japanese Targeting*.
2. This view is endorsed by President Ikehata of Spaulding Japan, who feels "you can't entirely ignore tradition. But don't get too hung up on customs. I'm a Japanese but I realize that to do something new you can't just say 'that's the way we've always done it.'" *Focus Japan*, March 1990, p. 8.
3. See Thomas Ainley, Jr., "Direct to the Heart," *Journal of the ACCJ*, June 1990, pp. 40–52.
4. For more ideas on how Japanese management can be outclassed, see Woronoff, *Japan's Wasted Workers*.
5. See MITI's *Gaishikei kigyo no doko* (Survey on Foreign-Affiliated Enterprises), annual.

Chapter 12 What now?

1. Kang, op. cit., p. 66.
2. On the Procter & Gamble story, see Huddleston, op. cit., pp. 185–92.
3. In some ways this ties up with Kang's third, and final, phase of becoming a "semi-insider." For more on what this entails and how it can be achieved, see Kang, op. cit., pp. 46–9 and 67–8.
4. For revealing insight into Japanese manufacturing, and what it signifies for foreign businessmen, see Kuniyasu Sakai, "The Feudal World of Japanese Manufacturing," *Harvard Business Review*, November–December 1990, pp. 38–49.
5. See Dodwell, *Industrial Groupings in Japan*, 1989, pp. 277–300.
6. On the reputed "successes" of foreign companies in Japan, see Christopher, op. cit.; Simon Collinson, *Small and Successful in Japan*; and Francis McIverney and Jean White, *Beating Japan*. On some failures, see James C. Abegglen and George Stalk, Jr., *Kaisha*, pp. 214–41.

Bibliography

1. Directories and Sourcebooks
2. Etiquette and Negotiating
3. Doing Business in Japan
4. Marketing and Distribution
5. Exporting, Joint Ventures, Acquisitions
6. Foreign Companies in Japan
7. Economic and Social Background
8. Japanese Management
9. Japanese Companies and Executives
10. *Keiretsu*, Groups and Trade Associations

1. Directories and sourcebooks

Gateway Japan, *Focus Japan. A Resource Guide to Japan-Oriented Organizations*, Washington, DC, Gateway Japan, 1993.

Guided Business Research, *Opportunity in Japan: The Kansai Area*, Osaka, GBR, 1996.

Japan External Trade Organization, *Directory for Doing Business in Japan*, Tokyo, JETRO, annual.

——, *Directory of Japanese Affiliated Companies in Asia*, Tokyo, JETRO, annual.

——, *Directory of Japanese Affiliated Companies in the USA and Canada*, Tokyo, JETRO, annual.

——, *Japan Trade Directory*, Tokyo, JETRO, annual.

——, *Manufacturing Technology Guide* (series), Tokyo, JETRO, periodic.

——, *Marketing Guidebook for Major Imported Products*, Tokyo, JETRO, annual.

——, *Standards Information* (series), Tokyo, JETRO, periodic.

——, *Trade Fairs in Japan*, Tokyo, JETRO, annual.

Toyo Keizai, *Japan Company Handbook, First Section*, Tokyo, Toyo Keizai, annual.

——, *Japan Company Handbook, Second Section*, Tokyo, Toyo Keizai, annual.

Yano Research Institute, *Market Share in Japan: A Comprehensive Guide to the Japanese Industrial Market*, Tokyo, Yano, annual.

Yellow Pages Japan in USA, *A Directory of Japanese Businesses in the USA and Canada*, Los Angeles, Yellow Pages Japan, annual.

2.   Etiquette and negotiating

Graham, John L. and Sano, Yoshihiro, *Smart Bargaining: Doing Business with the Japanese*, New York, Harper Business, 1989.

March, Robert M., *The Japanese Negotiator: Subtlety and Strategy Beyond Western Logic*, Tokyo and New York, Kodansha International.

Moran, Robert T., *Getting Your Yen's Worth: How To Negotiate with Japan, Inc.*, Houston, Gulf Publications, 1985.

Rowland, Diana, *Japanese Business Etiquette: a Practical Guide to Success with the Japanese*, New York, Warner Books, 1993.

Tung, Rosalie L., *Business Negotiations with the Japanese*, Lexington, DC, Heath, 1984.

Vardaman, James M., Jr. and Sasaki, Michiko, *Japanese Etiquette Today: A Guide to Business and Social Customs*, Rutland and Tokyo, Tuttle, 1994.

3. Doing business in Japan

Access Nippon, *Business Handbook How to Succeed in Japan*, Tokyo, Access Nippon, annual.

Alston, Jon P., *The Intelligent Businessman's Guide to Japan*, Rutland and Tokyo, Tuttle, 1990.

American Chamber of Commerce, *A Guide to Doing Business in Japan*, Tokyo, ACCJ, 1996.

Brannen, Christolyn, *Going to Japan on Business*, Berkeley, Bridge Press, 1997.

De Mente, Boye, *How To Do Business with the Japanese*, Chicago, NTC Publishing, 1987.

Engel, Dean and Murukami, Ken, *Passport Japan, Your Pocket Guide To Japanese Business, Customs and Etiquette*, San Rafael, World Trade Press, 1996.

Goldman, Alan, *Doing Business with the Japanese*, Albany, SUNY Press, 1994.

Hall, Edward T. and Reed, Mildred, *Hidden Differences: Doing Business with the Japanese*, Garden City, Anchor Press, 1987.

Huddleston, Jackson N., Jr., *Gaijin Kaisha, Running a Foreign Business in Japan*, Armonk, M.E. Sharpe, 1990.

James, David L., *Doing Business in Asia*, Cincinnati, Better Way Books, 1993.

Japan External Trade Organization, *Setting Up Enterprises in Japan*, 4th edn, Tokyo, JETRO, 1999.

Jung, Herbert F., *How to do Business with the Japanese*, Tokyo, Japan Times, 1986.

Lanier, Alison R., *The Rising Sun on Main Street: Working with the Japanese*, Yardley, International Information Associates, and Tokyo, Yohan, 1990.

Maurer, P. Reed, *Competing in Japan: Make It There, You Can Make It Anywhere*, Tokyo, Japan Times, 1989.

McAlinn, Gerald Paul (ed.), *The Business Guide to Japan*, Singapore, Butterworth-Heinemann Asia, 1996.

Metraux, Daniel Michael, *The Japanese Economy and the American Businessman*, Lewiston, Edwin Mellon Press, 1990.

Nevins, Thomas J., *Labor Pains and the Gaijin Boss*, Tokyo, Japan Times, 1983.

——, *Taking Charge in Japan*, Tokyo, Japan Times, 1990.

Thian, Helene, *Setting Up & Operating a Business in Japan*, Rutland and Tokyo, Tuttle, 1988.

Zimmerman, Mark, *How to do Business with the Japanese: A Strategy for Success*, New York, Random House, 1985.

4.   Marketing and distribution

Batzer, Eric and Laumer, Helmut, *Marketing Strategies and Distribution Channels for Foreign Companies in Japan*, Boulder, Westview, 1989.

Czinkota, Michael and Woronoff, Jon, *Unlocking Japan's Markets: Seizing Marketing and Distribution Opportunities in Today's Japan*, Chicago, Probus, 1991.

Dodwell Marketing Consultants, *Retail Distribution in Japan*, Tokyo, Dodwell, 1988.

Fields, George, *Gucci on the Ginza: Japan's New Consumer Generation*, Tokyo and New York, Kodansha International, 1989.

Japan External Trade Organization, *A Wealth of Opportunity, Japan's Distribution Channels*, Tokyo, JETRO, periodic.

Japan Machinery Importers' Association, *Japan as a Machinery Market*, Tokyo, JMIA, 1998.

Johanson, Johny K. and Ikujiro, Nonaka, *Relentless, The Japanese Way of Marketing*, New York, Harper Business, 1996.

Loughlin, Chuck and Sage, Karen, *Samurai Selling, The Ancient Art of Service in Sales*, New York, St. Martin's, 1995.

March, Robert M., *Honoring the Customer: Marketing and Selling to the Japanese*, New York, John Wiley, 1990.

Melville, Ian, *Marketing in Japan*, London, Butterworth-Heinemann, 1995.

5. Exporting, joint ventures, acquisitions

American Chamber of Commerce in Japan, *A Guide to Exporting to Japan*, Tokyo, ACCJ, 1995.

Gercik, Patricia, *On Trade with the Japanese: A Case-by-Case Approach to Building Successful Relationships*, Tokyo and New York, Kodansha International, 1996.

Hamada, Tomoko, *American Enterprise in Japan*, Albany, SUNY Press, 1991.

Ishizumi, Kanji, *Acquiring Japanese Companies: Mergers and Acquisitions in the Japanese Market*, Cambridge, Basil Blackwell, 1988.

Japan External Trade Organization, *Feasibility Study for Exporting to Japan*, Tokyo, JETRO, annual.

6.   Foreign companies in Japan

Christopher, Robert C., *Second to None: American Companies in Japan*, New York, Crown, 1986.

Collinson, Simon, *Small and Successful in Japan: A Study of Thirty British Firms in the World's Most Competitive Market*, Aldershot, Avebury, 1996.

Kang, T.W., *Gaishi: The Foreign Company in Japan*, New York, Basic Books, 1990.

Longworth, John W., *Beef in Japan: Politics, Production, Marketing and Trade*, St. Lucia, University of Queensland Press, 1983.

McIverney, Francis and White, Jean, *Beating Japan: How Hundreds of American Companies are Best in Japan Now and What Your Company Can Learn from Their Strategies and Success*, New York, Plume Books, 1994.

Morgan, James C. and Morgan, J. Jeffrey, *Cracking the Japanese Market*, New York, Free Press, 1991.

Raz, Aviad E., *Riding the Black Ship: Japan and Tokyo Disneyland*, Cambridge, MA, Harvard University Asia Center, 1998.

Watson, James L., *Golden Arches East: McDonald's in East Asia*, Stanford, Stanford University Press, 1997.

7. Economic and social background

Brown, Clair *et al.* (ed.), *Work and Pay in the United States and Japan*, New York, Oxford University Press, 1997.

Dattel, Eugene R., *The Sun That Never Rose: The Inside Story of Japan's Failed Attempt At Global Financial Dominance*, Chicago, Probus, 1994.

Fowler, Edward, *San'ya Blues: Laboring Life in Contemporary Tokyo*, Ithaca, Cornell University Press, 1997.

Gibney, Frank (ed.), *Unlocking the Bureaucrat's Kingdom: Deregulation and the Japanese Economy*, Washington, DC, Brookings Institution Press, 1998.

Katz, Richard, *Japan: The System that Soured: The Rise and Fall of the Japanese Economic Miracle*, Armonk, M.E. Sharpe, 1998.

Prestowitz, Clyde V., Jr., *Trading Places: How We Allowed Japan to Take the Lead*, New York, Basic Books, 1988.

Thurow, Lester, *Head to Head: The Coming Economic Battle Among Japan, Europe, and America*, New York, William Morrow, 1992.

Uriu, Robert M., *Troubled Industries: Confronting Economic Change in Japan*, Ithaca, Cornell University Press, 1996.

Woronoff, Jon, *The Japanese Economic Crisis*, 2nd edn, London, Macmillan, and New York, St. Martin's Press, 1996.

——, *The Japanese Social Crisis*, London, Macmillan, and New York, St. Martin's Press, 1997.

——, *World Trade War*, New York, Praeger, 1983.

8. Japanese management

Aoki, Masuhiko, *Information Incentives & Bargaining in the Japanese Economy*, New York, Cambridge University Press, 1988.

Aoki, Masahiko, and Dore, Ronald (eds), *The Japanese Firm, Sources of Competitive Strength*, Oxford, Clarendon Press, 1994.

Atarashi, Masami, *A Primer for Japanese Business Success*, Tokyo, Japan Times, 1994.

Ballon, Robert J. and Tomita, Iwao, *The Financial Behavior of Japanese Corporations*, Tokyo and New York, Kodansha International, 1988.

Beck, John C. and Martha N., *The Change of a Lifetime: Employment Patterns Among Japan's Management Elite*, Honolulu, University of Hawaii Press, 1994.

Belohlav, James A., *Championship Management*, Cambridge, MA, Productivity Press, 1990.

Durlabhji, Subhash and Marks, Norton E., *Japanese Business, Cultural Perspectives*, New York, SUNY Press, 1993.

Eli, Max, *Japan, Inc.: Global Strategies of Japanese Trading Corporations*, Chicago, Probus, 1991.

Hasegawa, Keitaro, *Japanese-Style Management: An Insider's Analysis*, Tokyo and New York, Kodansha International, 1986.

Hayashi, Shuji, *Culture and Management in Japan*, Tokyo, University of Tokyo Press, 1988.

Hunter, Janet E. (ed.), *Japanese Women Working*, London, Routledge, 1993.

Iizuku, Takeshi, *The Quest for Self: Zen in Business and Life*, New York, NYU Press, 1995.

Imai, Kenichi and Komiya, Ryutaro, *Business Enterprise in Japan*, Cambridge, MA, MIT Press, 1994.

Imai, Masaaki, *Kaizen, The Key to Japan's Competitive Success*, New York, McGraw-Hill, 1986.

Inoue, Shinishi, *Putting Buddhism to Work, A New Approach to Management and Business*, Tokyo and New York, Kodansha International, 1997.

Katchmer, George A., Jr., *Professional Budo, Ethics, Chivalry, and the Samurai Code of Lawyers, Doctors, and Managers*, Jamaica Plains, MA, YMAA Publications, 1995.

Kim, Byung Whan, *Seniority Wage System in the Far East*, Aldershot, Aveburg, 1992.

Koike, Kazuo, *Understanding Industrial Relations in Modern Japan*, New York, St. Martin's Press, 1988.

Kono, Toyohiro, *Strategy & Structure of Japanese Enterprises*, London, Macmillan, 1984.

Krause, Donald J., *Musashi's The Book of Five Rings for Executives*, London, Nicholas Brealey, 1998.

Kuboi, Takashi, *Business Practices and Taxation in Japan*, Tokyo, Japan Times, 1989.

Lo, Jeannie, *Office Ladies, Factory Women*, Armonk, M.E. Sharpe, 1990.

Lu, David J., *Inside Corporate Japan: The Art of Fumble-Free Management*, Stamford, CT, Productivity Press, 1987.

Ohmae, Kenichi, *The Mind of the Strategist: The Art of Japanese Business*, New York, McGraw Hill, 1982.

Schmincke, Don, *The Code of the Executive: Forty-Seven Ancient Samurai Principles Essential for Twenty-First Century Leadership Success*, Rutland, Tuttle, 1997.

Tatsuno, Sheridan M., *Created in Japan: From Imitators to World-Class Innovators*, New York, Harper & Row, 1990.

Thurow, Lester C. (ed.), *The Management Challenge, Japanese Views*, Cambridge, MA, MIT Press, 1992.

Woronoff, Jon, *Japan's Wasted Workers*, Chicago, Probus, 1991.

Yoshimura, Noboru and Anderson, Philip, *Inside the Kaisha: Demystifying Japanese Business Behavior*, Cambridge, MA, Harvard Business School Press, 1997.

Yuzawa, Takeshi (ed.), *Japanese Business Success: The Evolution of a Strategy*, London, Routledge, 1994.

9.   Japanese companies and executives

Barnett, Steve (ed.), *The Nissan Report: An Inside Look at How A World-Class Japanese Company Makes Products That Make A Difference*, New York, Doubleday Currency, 1992.

Fruin, W. Mark, *Knowledge Works: Managing Intellectual Capital at Toshiba*, New York, Oxford University Press, 1997.

Gould, Rowland, *The Matsushita Phenomenon*, Tokyo, Diamond Publishing, 1970.

Inamori, Kazuo, *For People and For Profit: A Business Philosophy for the 21st Century*, Tokyo and New York, Kodansha International, 1997.

——, *A Passion for Success*, New York, McGraw-Hill, 1995.

Kobayashi, Koji, *Rising to the Challenge*, Tokyo, Harcourt Brace Jovanovich Japan, 1989.

Kotten, John P., *Matsushita Leadership: Lessons from the 20th Century's Most Remarkable Entrepreneur*, New York, Free Press, 1997.

Kraar, Louis and Takikawa, Seiichi, *Japanese Maverick: Success Secrets of Canon's "God of Sales"*, New York, John Wiley, 1994.

NHK Group, *Good Mileage: The High-Performance Business Philosophy of Soichiro Honda*, Tokyo, NHK Publishing, 1996.

10. Keiretsu, groups and trade associations

Dodwell Marketing Consultants, *Industrial Groupings in Japan*, Tokyo, Dodwell, 1991.

Japan External Trade Organization, *Activities of Industrial Organizations in Japan*, Tokyo, JETRO, annual.

Lynn, Leonard H. and McKeown, Timothy J., *Organizing Business: Trade Associations in America and Japan*, Lanham, American Enterprise Institute, 1988.

Miyashita, Kenichi and Russell, David, *Keiretsu: Inside the Hidden Japanese Conglomerates*, New York, McGraw Hill, 1994.

Scher, Mark J., *Japanese Interfirm Networks and Their Main Banks*, Basingstoke, Macmillan, 1997.

Directory

Embassies

Australian Embassy
  2-1-14 Mita, Minato-ku, Tokyo 108
British Embassy
  1 Ichibancho, Chiyoda-ku, Tokyo 102
Canadian Embassy
  7-3-38 Akasaka, Minato-ku, Tokyo 107
French Embassy
  4-11-44 Minami-Azabu, Minato-ku, Tokyo 106
German Embassy
  4-5-10 Minami-Azabu, Minato-ku, Tokyo 106
New Zealand Embassy
  20-40 Kamiyamacho, Shibuya-ku, Tokyo 150
United States Embassy
  1-10-5 Akasaka, Minato-ku, Tokyo 107

Foreign chambers

American Chamber of Commerce
  Bridgestone Toranomon Bldg., 3-25-2 Toranomon, Minato-ku, Tokyo 105
Australia & New Zealand Chamber of Commerce
  New Otani Garden Court 28F, 4-1 Kioicho, Chiyoda-ku, Tokyo 102
British Chamber of Commerce
  Kenkyusha Eigo Center Bldg. 3F, 1-2 Kagurazaka, Shinjuku-ku, Tokyo 162
Canadian Chamber of Commerce
  Chez Irene Bldg. 2F, 7-4-7 Akasaka, Minato-ku, Tokyo 107
French Chamber of Commerce
  Iida Bldg., 5-5 Rokubancho, Chiyoda-ku, Tokyo 102
German Chamber of Commerce & Industry
  KS Bldg. 5F, 2 Sanbancho, Chiyoda-ku, Tokyo 102

Japanese organizations

Japan Chamber of Commerce & Industry
  Tosho Bldg., 3-2-2 Marunouchi, Chiyoda-ku, Tokyo 100
Japan External Trade Organizations (JETRO)
  2-5 Toranomon 2-chome, Minato-ku, Tokyo 105
JETRO, Frankfurt
  Rossmark 17, 60311 Frankfurt, Germany

JETRO, Hong Kong
  1910 Hutchison house, 10 Harcourt Road, Central, Hong Kong, China.
JETRO, London
  Leconfield House, Curzon Street, London W1Y 7FB, United Kingdom
JETRO, New York
  McGraw-Hill Bldg., 44th Floor, 1221 Avenue of the Americas, New York,
  NY 10020, United States
JETRO, Paris
  151 bis Rue Saint-Honoré, 75001 Paris, France
JETRO, Sydney
  Gateway Bldg. I, Level 19, Macquarie Place, Sydney, NSW 2000, Australia
Japan Federation of Economic Organizations (Keidanren)
  1-9-4 Otemachi, Chiyoda-ku, Tokyo 100
Manufactured Imports Promotion Organization
  World Import Mart Building, 6th Floor, 3-1-3 Higashi Ikebukuro, Toshima-
  ku, Tokyo 170
Ministry of International Trade & Industry (MITI)
  1-3-1 Kasumigaseki, Chiyoda-ku, Tokyo 100

Index